Praise for other b

The Coaching Manual

Widely recognised as a leading practical handbook on coaching, *The Coaching Manual* combines an understanding of coaching principles, skills, attitudes and behaviours, along with practical guidance and a comprehensive toolkit for coaches.

The Coaching Manual demystifies the full coaching process, from first step to final meeting. This is the complete guide to coaching and includes models, perspectives, skills, case studies, tips and advice.

Praise for *The Coaching Manual* includes:

> *The Coaching Manual is the most current, comprehensive practical and best-illustrated source I have ever seen. It compellingly teaches the mind-set of keeping the responsibility on the coach combined with a powerful, realistic skill set.*

> **Dr Stephen R. Covey, author of**
> ***The 7 Habits of Highly Effective People***

> *The most comprehensive book on the practice of coaching that I have come across. If anyone wishes to become a one-to-one coach and only read one book about it, this could well be that book.*

> **Sir John Whitmore, Executive Chairman,**
> **Performance Consultants International**
> **and author of *Coaching for Performance***

Brilliant Coaching 2011, Harlow: Pearson Education

Coaching is fast becoming the must-have leadership skill and this book shows how anyone can become a brilliant coach at work. Based on methods specifically developed and proven in business, you will discover what it takes to be a coach, how to use the core coaching methods and how to apply these to common coaching scenarios.

Containing simple, practical ways to becoming a brilliant coach at work, you will be able to unlock your unique coaching ability and reap the rewards in no time at all.

Praise for *Brilliant Coaching* includes:

> *Extremely effective tips on coaching principles backed up by true-to-life examples and exercises throughout. A 'brilliant' tool for success.*

Dr Stephen R. Covey, author of
The 7 Habits of Highly Effective People

The
Mentoring
Manual

The Mentoring Manual

Your step by step guide to
being a better mentor

Julie Starr

PEARSON

Harlow, England • London • New York • Boston • San Francisco • Toronto • Sydney
Auckland • Singapore • Hong Kong • Tokyo • Seoul • Taipei • New Delhi
Cape Town • São Paulo • Mexico City • Madrid • Amsterdam • Munich • Paris • Milan

PEARSON EDUCATION LIMITED
Edinburgh Gate
Harlow CM20 2JE
United Kingdom
Tel: +44 (0)1279 623623
Web: www.pearson.com/uk

First published 2014 (print and electronic)

© Pearson Education Limited 2014 (print and electronic)

The right of Julie Starr to be identified as author of this work has been asserted by her
in accordance with the Copyright, Designs and Patents Act 1988.
Pearson Education is not responsible for the content of third-party internet sites.

ISBN: 978-1-292-01789-1 (print)
         978-1-292-01791-4 (PDF)
         978-1-292-01792-1 (ePub)
         978-1-292-01790-7 (eText)

British Library Cataloguing-in-Publication Data
A catalogue record for the print edition is available from the British Library

Library of Congress Cataloging-in-Publication Data
A catalog record for the print edition is available from the Library of Congress

Cover design: Rob Day
Print edition typeset in 9.5pt Giovanni by 30

NOTE THAT ANY PAGE CROSS REFERENCES REFER TO THE PRINT EDITION

Contents

About the author

Julie Starr is an executive coach, mentor, writer and speaker. She works with individuals and organisations to help them clarify a sense of purpose and remove obstacles to progress.

Author of two best-selling books on coaching, *The Coaching Manual* and *Brilliant Coaching*, Julie is also a passionate advocate of mentoring. She says:

'Mentoring isn't about changing someone, or getting someone to do something differently, it's about waking someone up to who they really are. The mentor's challenge is to distil their own experience into bite-sized chunks of wisdom, help or guidance in ways that ultimately help them to discover that.'

Author's acknowledgements

This book has been guided, shaped and supported by so many wonderful teachers. I am especially grateful for the work and contribution of the following people – all of whom have served as my mentors in some way – Mata Amritanandamayi, Brandon Bays, Kevin Billet, Rev. Birch ret., Dr Stephen Covey, Eckhart Tolle, Sir John Whitmore and Mr Whittorn (my wonderful, inspiring English teacher).

I would also like to thank my editor Eloise Cook for her encouragement to write this book, and Dr Xanthe Wells for her assistance in the production of the text.

Introduction

This book offers you a comprehensive guide to support your thinking as a mentor, as well as helping you decide what to do and how to do it. From preparing to mentor someone, to the ultimate completion of the relationship, you will find explanation, advice and 'how-to' type guidance to help you embark upon and maintain a confident course. Chapters 1 to 4 explain what mentoring is and identify the principles that define and shape the distinct nature of the role. Chapter 5 offers you a practical process to support and guide you in your role as mentor, so if you're keen to get started, then perhaps check that out early on. You can then return to the earlier chapters to build your awareness and deepen your understanding. Chapter 6 will give you some examples of pitfalls to watch out for along the way. If you want an overview of the key messages in all of the chapters, you'll find that in Chapter 7.

A mentor provides support by offering information, advice and assistance in a way that empowers the mentee

Mentoring is a distinct relationship where one person (the mentor) supports the learning, development and progress of another person (the mentee). A mentor provides support by offering information, advice and assistance in a way that empowers the mentee. Many of us are familiar with the term mentoring, but I wonder how often we overlook its true potential as something we might explore for ourselves. For example, did you know that it's very likely you already have relationships in which you adopt the role of a mentor? Or that to become a great mentor you already have much of the ability you need? So why not hone these existing skills to become sharper and more effective?

Mentoring is a rich source of self-learning and personal growth. It offers you the opportunity to make a tangible difference to the success of others. This might be to help increase their confidence or ability, or support their career success. When our enjoyment comes from the difference we make to other people, mentoring becomes a living definition of the term 'win-win'.

This book will help you answer the following questions:

- What is mentoring and how is it distinct from other types of relationship?
- What does becoming a better mentor mean to you, e.g. what are the benefits?
- What areas do you need to focus on to become a better mentor, e.g. behaviours, principles and process?
- How can you start practising these principles right away?
- What are your unseen 'barriers' or 'blocks' to effective mentoring, e.g. beliefs, behaviours or circumstances? How can you overcome them?

First let's take a quick look at how you can get the most from the book.

The mentoring 'journey'

A mentoring relationship can be likened to the idea of a journey, i.e. an experience where you set out to go somewhere, travel for a while, overcome hazards and diversions, and ultimately reach somewhere else. Throughout the book, you will notice journey-type language to illustrate this: 'navigate', 'path', 'destination', etc. Journeys are a constant part of our lives, so this instinctive, familiar sense of physical travel can help us to relate to the more interpretative experience of mentoring. Every now and then I'll use the journey metaphor more specifically and you might like to visualise your own imagery to complement this. For now, let's start with equipping yourself for travel.

A book that works in collaboration with you

This book is based on three main ideas. If you allow these ideas to guide your mentoring journey, then you will be naturally inclined to accept, adapt and incorporate concepts in ways that benefit you. While you don't have to live the rest of your life by these concepts, it will help if you accept them for now, at least on a logical level, e.g. 'I understand the sense of that and I can agree with it'.

Idea One: Some things can be taught and others must be learned

The basis for the 'teaching' element of this book comes from what I've learned from professionally coaching and mentoring others. Your part in this is to work with the ideas and information in ways that are practical for you. That means keeping reading and working with the ideas, trying out the exercises and checklists, etc. Ultimately, you will decide what you agree or disagree with in a way that works for you.

Idea Two: While all journeys benefit from a sense of destination and purpose, no great adventure was ever planned in detail

It helps to have an open mind about what mentoring might be for you and what you might ultimately do with this topic. For example, you might feel that mentoring is something you should know more about so that you can talk confidently about it. Or perhaps you are interested for professional reasons and have little interest in how it relates to relationships outside of work. Whatever your motivations for picking up the book, you will achieve more if you are willing to expand and adapt them along the way. If you imagine that you simply need to acquire knowledge, or pick up some handy hints and tips, then you are likely to do only that. However, if you acknowledge that this topic is one you are willing to look into with an open mind, you might reveal more about yourself than you expected.

Idea Three: Anything worth having is worth working for

In a world where 'quick and easy' seems to be on offer every-where, the universal truth remains that anything in your life of value to you will require effort to acquire, maintain or enhance. What you value is up to you, e.g. a great car, your favourite people or your health. Sometimes we value something more because of our endeavours to obtain it; conversely, we might value something less simply because it has felt 'too easy'. This is neither right nor wrong, just part of being human.

As you read, sometimes you will be required to do something extra, do something differently or consider something from another perspective. It is our mind's natural tendency to want to stay in control, perhaps by saying 'Yes, I know that already' or 'That's awkward so I'll ignore it' or 'Yes, I should do that but I'll do it when I have more time'. Unfortunately this tendency directly impairs our ability to enquire, learn and create positive change. As author Neal Donald Walsch says:

Life begins at the end of your comfort zone.

Simply, what is required is that you stay aware of these limiting tendencies or beliefs while you are reading. For example, if you notice that you're enjoying reading the ideas but skipping the exercises, perhaps go back and try one of the exercises that feels 'less easy'. It's quite possible that you will gain as much from a ten-minute exercise as an hour spent reading the book. So please allow the three concepts to help you to benefit as you read and know that you can, of course, return to or withdraw from them at any point. Think of them as preparation for your journey: a useful map to guide and support you, but one that you can put back in your pocket when you feel comfortable to do that.

It's quite possible that you will gain as much from a ten-minute exercise as an hour spent reading the book

No jacket required

I will often talk to you as though you already are a manager and/ or mentor. Please know that you do not have to be a mentor or a manager to benefit from the ideas in this book. If you are in any situation where helping others to learn, grow and develop would really help (them or you), I'm confident that this book has something to offer. If you are mentoring as part of a mentoring scheme, e.g. run by your organisation or company, please let the book add to the existing principles and guidance you already have available to you.

As you read, you'll notice bite-sized sections that support your practice and learning. When you use them, these items will help you to increase both your self-awareness and your ability to mentor others. These sections comprise the following.

Reflection questions

These are a series of questions to help you link ideas specifically to your own situation and reflect on them to gain personal insight. You can write down your answers, speak them out loud, or just pause and think them through. The important thing to remember is that the questions are intended to provoke thought and action. By pausing and attending to the questions, you're letting the book go to work for you.

Checklists

These are quick summaries of points to confirm your understanding and also serve as memory joggers for future reference – for example, to remind you of things you can do to build respect in the relationship, or how you'll know you've had a constructive first session.

Story Teller

These are fictional examples to illustrate a principle or idea and use imaginary situations and people. They are inspired by my own work in this area, and are sometimes real situations combined to use features of both/all of them. Here I am also demonstrating a key technique you can use to mentor others, namely to tell stories from your own experience.

Exercise

At intervals, you'll be asked to try an approach or routine in a situation, such as an everyday conversation. This is where you will begin to make progress on your ability to mentor others more effectively. Some exercises will be straightforward and help you confirm your understanding, while others will challenge you to do something a little further from your comfort zone.

Hints and tips

These tips are a quick visual reminder of hints or advice to remind you of key points – for example, what to remember during conversations with your mentee, or how to balance talking with listening. Like the rest of the inserts, they are a quick visual aid that you can go back to at any time.

Mentor's toolkit: available online

To help you in your everyday mentoring, I have compiled downloadable content on my website at www.starrconsulting.co.uk. Here you will find documents to support your effectiveness as a mentor, including an overview of mentoring to give to someone you are preparing to mentor, and an agenda for a first meeting. This content is free to use as part of your personal practice and I request that you do not charge others for it.

Chapter summary

Becoming an effective mentor requires us to stay as engaged in our own development and learning as we hope the people we intend to mentor will. As in life, you will get out of this book what you put into it and that's a good thing, because it gives you the direct ability to influence your own results, success and enjoyment. You already have existing ability and potential to be a great mentor for others – all you need to do is explore and build on that.

Chapter

1

I worked with Laurence Olivier some years ago.
He was a great mentor.

Anthony Hopkins, actor

What is mentoring?
And what is it not?

In this chapter:

- Gain a clearer sense of what a mentor is.
- Learn how mentoring is distinct from any other support relationship.
- Consider examples of mentors from stories and real life to support your understanding of the role.
- Discover the typical benefits of mentoring, both for individuals and for organisations.
- Understand when mentoring might not be the best option for a situation.

What is a mentor?

A mentor is someone who takes on the role of a trusted adviser, supporter, teacher and wise counsel to another person. A mentor adopts a primarily selfless role in supporting the learning, development and ultimate success of another person. By 'primarily selfless' I mean that while as a mentor you will often benefit in some way from the relationship, these benefits are usually indirect and not your main motivation for mentoring someone. You might easily enjoy your mentoring sessions and gain skills, awareness and insight from doing that. However, mentoring is most effective when focused clearly on the needs, goals and challenges of the person you are mentoring – often referred to as the 'mentee'.

As old as Homer's *Odyssey*

Mentoring can often be defined by the nature and intention of a relationship. The term 'mentor' has its roots in Greek mythology and indicates a relationship of support, help and guidance given from a wise elder to a younger, less experienced person. This idea of 'passing down wisdom' has been embedded in cultures for thousands of years and can be seen in relationships both inside and outside the workplace. The consistent features of mentor relationships distinguish an archetype for the role. By archetype, I mean typical models or examples of the role which can inform our understanding. While situations and appearances may vary, the essential qualities remain. Consider the fictional teacher Miss Jean Brodie offering wise counsel to her school girls, or *The X Factor* judges mentoring their performers – can you see common features in those relationships? From community mentors working with youth, to business mentoring, young offender programmes or apprenticeships in skilled trades, the ancient archetype of a mentor is brought to life all around us.

Indeed, the mentor archetype is so constantly present in our lives that its powerful principles can remain unseen. For example, the principle that by forming an open, trusting relationship with someone, we create a channel through which support, help and learning can happen is something we have all experienced. Think back: did you sometimes listen to the advice of your grandparents more readily than that of your parents? Or was there someone else you might say that about? Most of us can recall someone we might now recognise was a mentor for us in the past.

Reflection Questions	

Spot your own mentors

Use the following Reflection Questions to identify relationships you had/have that might have been mentoring.

Q. Thinking about your childhood and growing up, who had a positive influence on how you see the world?

Q. In your youth, was there a particular teacher, relation or friend who you would credit with having taught you lessons in life you are grateful for?

Q. During your career, who has had a positive influence on how you operate professionally?

Q. Who would you generally credit as being your mentors in life?

Q. What relationships do you have right now that appear to fit the criteria of mentorship, e.g. someone you respect, someone you learn from, a relationship that feels 'personal' in a positive way?

Why might you want to be a mentor?

There are countless benefits available in becoming a mentor, many unforeseen and unexpected. From my experience, mentoring people can be challenging, fulfilling, gratifying, annoying, frustrating, impossible and fun – all in the same relationship! Reasons that you might consider mentoring others include:

- to affirm or confirm the value of your experience by exploring and sharing that with someone else, e.g. 'Here's what I've learned'
- to further clarify what you know, by distilling and simplifying your experience and learning, e.g. 'Here's what leadership/selling/success is really about'
- to help another person grow and succeed, and gain a sense of satisfaction from doing that
- to be challenged in a positive way. For example, to adapt your ideas or views to someone else's situations, or to develop greater empathy
- to have a sense of 'giving something back', perhaps by sharing experience gained over your career so far
- to increase your focus on developing others, as a useful addition to your managing skills. For example, as a mentor

you have no line management responsibility for the person you are mentoring, therefore you tend to focus more on the person and less on their specific tasks.

Mentoring people can be challenging, fulfilling, gratifying, annoying, frustrating, impossible and fun

Why might someone want a mentor?

Reasons for seeking a mentor are both personal and professional. An individual may want a mentor for one or more of these reasons:

- They feel they lack experience, contacts or awareness in a specific area or situation, e.g. 'I need to understand business start-ups, or how my organisation works, or to raise my profile in the business'.

- They feel something is 'missing' from what they know, what they do or how they think, and they want to learn from someone they feel can help them 'bridge a gap'.

- They want to mature and develop themselves generally, e.g. to be able to operate in a pressurised work environment or stay balanced and self-confident.

- They have reached some kind of barrier or 'roadblock' and feel they need a more individualised relationship with someone who has direct experience in their type of situation.

- They feel they would benefit from an open, trusting relationship with someone they can 'look up to' or at least respect for what they have experienced and learned during their career.

How did the idea of the mentor evolve?

The original 'Mentor' appeared in Homer's book *The Odyssey*, as an old and trusted friend of Odysseus. As he left to go to war, Odysseus entrusted Mentor with the care of his son, Telemachus.

Later, the goddess Athena took on the appearance of Mentor and used the disguise to give advice and practical guidance to both Odysseus and his son. Athena knew that because they had such trust and respect for Mentor, they would follow her advice more easily. Since then the idea of a mentoring role has appeared in many stories and fables, including those portrayed in novels, the theatre and film. Traditionally, the mentor archetype includes attributes of tutorship, learning and sometimes even magic or transformation.

When we attempt to define the mentor role only by behaviour, we can get confused by potential contradictions. For example, if a mentor is supposed to give advice, does that mean they do not help another person to think for themselves, perhaps by asking 'What are your options here?' or 'What do you want to do?' Or, if a mentor is supposed to provide assistance, how much help is too much help?

It's useful to explore the concept of a mentor by returning to the original archetype: the source of the concept can give you a stronger sense of what the role might mean for you. When your understanding is guided by the original concept, such as 'a mentor shares wisdom to foster learning and progress', then 'how' you express that becomes a question of personal choice. It might include giving clear advice, or it may be expressed by telling stories or even jokes. In Chapter 3, we will examine further principles from the original mentor archetype to show how they can help guide our choices in situations.

Reflection Questions

Where are you already a mentor?

Use the following Reflection Questions to identify current relationships where you might be already expressing the characteristics of a mentor.

Q. Outside of your immediate family, e.g. your partner, children, etc., what relationships are you aware of where someone values your views and opinions and can often be influenced by those?

▶

Q. How much does this person appear to respect you, or even look up to you?

Q. Think about how you relate to them, e.g. how much affinity or benevolence (generosity) do you feel towards them?

Where your answers to the second two questions confirm the presence of respect and benevolence, it's likely you are expressing mentoring principles in the relationship. However, if your responses to the second two questions are in disagreement, then the relationship is less likely to be a mentoring type of relationship.

Translating fable to fact

Even though our inspiration for the mentor archetype is mythical, the links to a modern-day mentor relationship are fairly straightforward:

- The person being mentored (the mentee) has something that they desire or want to achieve – perhaps to gain something, such as learning, confidence or a sense of clarity, or reach an external goal such as promotion or financial reward.
- A mentor has knowledge, experience and perhaps opinion/ insight in areas of value to the mentee, e.g. business start-ups, running teams or simply career success.
- A mentor has a level of maturity around a topic that enables them to offer views and opinions based on understanding. For example, they have run various teams, during times of ease and difficulty, which enables them to comment upon principles of managing teams effectively.

To remind you of the essential qualities of a mentor, and mentor relationships, check Table 1.1.

Table 1.1 Mentor–mentee relationships in the movies

Mentor	Mentee	Source
Saul Berenson	Carrie Mathison	*Homeland*
Karen Brady	The contestants	*The Apprentice*
Professor Dumbledore	Harry Potter	*Harry Potter*
Arthur Fonzarelli	Richie Cunningham	*Happy Days*
Gandalf	Frodo Baggins	*Lord of the Rings*
Hagrid	Harry Potter	*Harry Potter*
Tom Jones	The contestants	*The Voice*
Mister Miyagi	Daniel	*The Karate Kid*
Ser Jorah Mormont	Daenerys Targaryen	*Game of Thrones*
Obi-Wan Kenobi	Luke Skywalker	*Star Wars*
Mary Poppins	Jane and Michael Banks	*Mary Poppins*
Proximo	Maximus Decimus Meridius	*Gladiator*
Nicole Scherzinger	The contestants	*The X Factor*
Oprah Winfrey	Women in general	*The Oprah Winfrey Show*
Willy Wonka	Charlie Bucket	*Charlie and the Chocolate Factory*

Reflection Questions

Confirm progress

Use the following Reflection Questions to increase your personal sense of what it means to be a mentor.

Q. What do the previous mentor characters seem to have in common?

Q. Many of the mentors illustrated have some element of 'mystery' or 'dubious past'. How could this be relevant for a mentor now, i.e. why is it a useful idea to consider?

Q. What questions do you have that you still need to answer?

When you're mature enough, you're old enough

Some aspects of the ancient archetype are less practical than others and these have been relaxed over time. For example, being older than a mentee by one or more generations is now less a clear attribute of a mentor than experience, awareness or skill. This is possibly because age does not assure wisdom, nor does youth always indicate a lack of it. There is no such thing as the 'optimum age for a mentor', nor is there a minimum number of years' seniority between a mentor and their mentee. While it is logical to assume becoming experienced takes time (meaning that a mentor is likely to be older), what actually qualifies you as a mentor might be more about life experience, relevant knowledge or general maturity.

Age does not assure wisdom, nor does youth always indicate a lack of it

Checklist

Features of a modern-day mentor

Using the original mentor archetype as a base, we can assume that a mentor role includes the following:

✔ A relationship where one person (the mentee) is learning from another (the mentor).

✔ The mentor is appropriate to support an individual because the mentor has knowledge, skills or experience that are relevant to that person's situations and goals.

✔ The mentor has a series of conversations with their mentee that usefully relate to the mentee's situations and goals.

✔ The mentor feels a degree of benevolence towards the mentee – they would like to see them succeed.

✔ The mentor is someone whom the mentee respects in a way that enables them to be influenced by them, i.e. it is not necessary for the mentee to 'like' the mentor.

✔ The mentee is the person who aims to be developed or to gain most directly from the relationship.

✔ While the relationship has no fixed duration, there may be a period of time over which the relationship is most relevant and therefore most active.

How do organisations use mentoring?

Mentoring has been used for many years to mature and develop individuals, and the use of mentoring continues to grow. By 2013, according to Adecco Employment Agency, 79 per cent of workplaces offered internal mentoring schemes. Also, in the 2013 CIPD (The Chartered Institute of Personnel and Development) Learning and Talent Development Survey, mentoring is listed by organisations as one of their top missing leadership skills. Clearly, while organisations are actively mentoring, they are also indicating a desire to get better at that.

Mentoring is seen as a way of nurturing talent and also a way to develop the skills of the people who are mentoring others. Here are just a few of the reasons why organisations encourage mentoring:

- to develop people in specific areas, e.g. leadership, working cross-culturally, commercial acumen, etc.

- to support people new to a role or transitioning to a new situation
- to nurture and foster talent, e.g. broaden people's knowledge and understanding, help to mature more junior professionals
- to groom/position individuals to succeed key people and so reduce the risk of loss of those people (as part of a succession-planning process)
- to help individuals through a challenging period, e.g. returning to work after extended absence
- to provide individuals with support in the absence of a line manager, e.g. when they are working in a resource pool
- to provide development and learning for individuals in the absence of other options, e.g. attendance on costly training courses, executive coaching, etc.

Use of mentoring schemes

Mentoring can be used in isolated situations for specific individuals, e.g. individuals thought to be high potential and in need of development. In addition, some organisations build mentoring schemes that involve groups of mentors operating from a set of agreed principles and processes. For further discussion of mentoring schemes, see Chapter 5, 'A process to support your journey'.

An individual may be assigned a mentor from inside or outside their organisation. For example, where the organisation seeks to give someone experience of a specific kind, or broaden someone's view of how the business operates, they may match them to someone inside their organisation. Where they want to grow someone's industry knowledge, they might seek a seasoned professional outside of the company network, perhaps sourcing that mentor through their network of contacts, a mentoring agency, or a professional body that supports mentoring. One example of this is the mentor programme offered by the Institution of Mechanical Engineers (IMechE), where developing engineers are matched to volunteer mentors outside of their organisation (see www.imeche.org for more details).

Using internal and external mentoring to promote the employer brand

A high-street clothes retailer wanted to demonstrate their commitment to developing staff and provide them with a clearer sense of career progression. They also wanted to develop their ability to keep pace with the changing nature of high-street retailing, e.g. customer expectations, social trends, technology, etc. An internal mentoring scheme was established to support and develop new and recently joined managers to help them 'survive and thrive' during a potentially tough initial 18-month period. Managers who had longer service were also considered for the internal mentoring scheme but had the added potential to be assigned an external mentor instead.

External mentors were identified from both within the retail sector and outside of it. For example, mentors were found from mobile phone retailers, restaurant chains and a hotel group. This mentoring by professionals outside of the company helped the managers to broaden their outlook and also to challenge their thinking about their approach to business, innovations in the marketplace, the customer experience, etc.

The combination of methods was monitored to understand the benefits of both options (mentoring by people who were internal and external to the company). In this way, over time the retailer was able to increase the effectiveness of the 'matching' process, i.e. how to decide if a manager would benefit more from an external mentor or one from inside the company instead.

How does mentoring compare with coaching, training and consultancy?

The potential similarities between coaching, training and consultancy demand that we reflect more generally to decide the relative differences of each. Table 1.2 indicates some initial features of the various activities to illustrate some obvious and simple differences.

Table 1.2 Mentoring, coaching, training, consultancy: the differences

Activity	Typical features and attributes	Who is expected to have responsibility for learning, development and change?
Mentoring	Delivered by someone with a relevant set of skills, experience and perspectives, e.g. 'I am a working mum involved in education for ten years and three of those have been spent in Asia.' The mentor is mostly interested in the person and the content of the conversations, whereas coaches and trainers will additionally focus on the process of learning.	The mentee is expected to be responsible for their own learning; however, the mentor may also take on some secondary sense of responsibility for that. This shared sense of responsibility is often dependent on the nature of the individual mentor, e.g. a willingness to become involved. The mentor will not normally be held accountable in any way for the mentee's results, but will often receive feedback on their effectiveness, e.g. as part of a company-wide Mentor Scheme.
Coaching	Delivered by someone with training in how to coach others, e.g. to use skills of listening, questioning and facilitation to assist people to think and act for themselves. A coach focuses on the process of coaching conversations, in addition to the person and their situations.	The person being coached (the coachee) is encouraged to be responsible for their own learning. However, the coach will normally be evaluated on their effectiveness, e.g. how skilled are they at facilitating change? So while the coach is not responsible, they may be wise to feel accountable.

Training	Delivered to individuals and groups by someone with the ability to deliver training and also with theory and knowledge of the topic on which they are delivering training, e.g. presentation skills, project management, interviewing skills, etc. Effective trainers understand different approaches to encouraging learning/development and will be creative with those – for example, blending group work with individual exercises, or knowing how to maintain energy, engagement and interest.	Responsibility for the transfer of learning begins with the trainer, who is expected to design and deliver effective training. This responsibility later becomes shared with the learner as they are expected to engage with the training process, e.g. attend classes, do follow-up work, etc. A trainer will often be judged on their ability to deliver training that affects a person's learning and ability, plus hopefully their behaviours or behavioural style.
Consultancy	Consultancy services are normally delivered by someone who has relevant knowledge and experience, plus structured methods/tools for improving business practices – for example, knowledge of implementing safety within a construction environment, or of improving productivity, costs or business results. Their involvement will often be targeted at situations, rather than people, and they will endeavour to maintain an impartial, detached view, e.g. 'What's the best overall solution here?'	The consultant is regularly judged on their ability to effect improvement and change and so needs to maintain a sense of responsibility (and accountability) for the results of their involvement. However, the consultant's success in encouraging change relates directly to their ability to engage people or to create a shared sense of the situation with the people they are working with – for example, they must encourage the client and the client teams to buy-into or engage with, any proposed approach.

Blending theory with reality

Organisations might use mentoring where their resources do not stretch to another solution, e.g. training and consultancy. In this case, we may find ourselves straying from the traditional understanding of a mentor role, i.e. to fulfil the mentee's actual needs. For example, we may help rehearse a mentee through a presentation and 'teach' them presentation skills, because if we didn't, no one else would. In any potential 'situational dilemma' it is important that the mentor operates from a clear set of principles that helps guide their decisions. In the next chapter, 'What's different about a mentoring relationship?', we will look more closely at the principles and values from which a mentor operates.

When does mentoring become coaching or managing?

Where the organisation has a specific agenda for the mentoring that is not something that both the mentor and the mentee are engaged in, this can dilute the integrity of the mentor role. By 'integrity' I mean the pure (and powerful) intentions of the role, arising from the simple principles that underpin it. Perhaps the organisation would like the mentor to improve the performance of the mentee. This revised role, where the mentor is given objectives related to performance and results, leans more towards the intentions of managing or coaching. This is because responsibility and implied accountability have shifted (from the mentee to the mentor). Remember also that a mentor is not responsible or accountable for the performance of an individual – this is something a manager is focused on.

A mentor is not responsible or accountable for the performance of an individual

Story Teller

Adapting the mentor role can be a valid response to the needs of the individual and the organisation

An IT company employed software engineers to work on projects to help build or adapt software applications. The engineers were assigned to work as part of a project team, typically for a six-month period, and then they moved to a different project and team. During a project, an engineer's 'manager' was the manager of the project they were assigned to. This Project Manager was interested only in the engineer's performance during the project (because that's what the Project Manager was accountable for). The engineers had no manager in the traditional sense, e.g. someone who would focus on their performance over time, discuss their development needs, etc.

The engineers needed additional support that included a focus on their long-term performance and their career. They also needed someone they could go to if they were having issues that they were unable to discuss with the Project Manager (such as a concern over career options, or training needs). In response, the IT company created a hybrid mentor role, i.e. a modified version of the role to meet the engineers' needs. Taking the original principles of the mentor role, they adapted it. For example:

- They encouraged mentoring conversations to focus on specific topics, such as career development or the need to identify training and development needs.
- They specified the duration of a mentor's involvement as a minimum of 18 months, to encourage a longer-term relationship to develop.
- They requested that mentoring conversations occurred at least once every 6–8 weeks to ensure that mentees felt they had access to regular support.

▶

Mentees (the engineers) were still responsible for their own learning; however, the mentors were expected to raise certain topics in support of their on-going performance and development.

It was important to scope both the Project Manager's and the mentor's role carefully, to assign clear involvement and accountability. For example:

- The mentor did not conduct the engineer's annual appraisal conversation, at which they would receive feedback, be given a performance rating and also potentially receive a bonus.

- The mentor did contribute towards the appraisal conversation, by summarising (in a document) the feedback they had previously offered their mentee as part of their regular conversations.

- The mentor's documented feedback was shared first with the mentee (the engineer) and later the panel of two/three Project Managers assigned to conduct their appraisal conversation. This gave the mentee time to respond to the feedback, e.g. understand or challenge messages as appropriate.

While this is not a typical or 'authentic' use of the mentor role, it is justified as a valid response to the needs of the organisation and the individuals who work there.

Be clear about how and why you have reshaped the mentor role

As shown in the previous story, a dilution or reshaping of a 'pure' mentor's role can be appropriate in some situations. Here are some of the ways of creating a positive sense of balance to explain and even promote the need for a revised approach:

- Explain the nature and intentions of the role openly to all parties: the mentor, the mentee, the mentee's manager, etc.

- Communicate the rationale for the revised approach, such as:
  - 'We need to accelerate people's development in some areas critical to our overall plan (such as safety, data protection, innovation, etc.).'
- Consider a more accurate name for the role, e.g. 'coach mentor' or 'manager coach'.

Reshaping the mentor role can sometimes be a mistake

Reshaping the mentor role to accommodate additional needs and opportunities can seem like a simple and straightforward thing to do, e.g. 'Let's get the training function to ask the mentor what courses their mentee should go on.' However, with every adaptation of the mentor role comes some kind of compromise for that role. For example, when we ask the mentor what training they think their mentee needs, we also:

- reduce their impartiality (as they must 'judge' their mentee)
- give them subtle responsibility for the mentee's learning
- create a potential perception with a mentee of inequality, e.g. 'They are deciding something for me' or 'They have power over me.'

With every adaptation of the mentor role comes some kind of compromise for that role

Here are situations where it is less appropriate to corrupt the integrity of the role, for instance by adding in 'manager type' of involvement and responsibility:

- where the justification for this is that the mentee's current manager lacks the time, skills or motivation to focus on someone's performance and development
- where it has not been made clear to all parties that this will happen, i.e. the mentee or manager is unaware of this
- where the mentor does not have the time or skills to adapt their focus, e.g. to support someone's performance or delivery

- where the implications of doing this have not been properly explored, e.g. 'If the mentor decides someone's performance-related bonus – how does that impact openness in the conversations?'

When is mentoring not the best option?

Sometimes, mentoring is not the best solution, depending on the situation and what's needed. Table 1.3 illustrates the main considerations in a situation to help you judge which intervention (mentoring, coaching, consultancy, etc.) will work best.

Table 1.3 Different options for different situations

Situation	Requirements/ Objectives	Recommendation
An experienced team of 12 people has returned employee opinion surveys to indicate a lack of satisfaction in leadership generally. Further analysis indicates a senior manager is the target for individual criticism. The most obvious cause appears to be a lack of appropriately skilled leadership and/or burnout.	• To understand and tackle the main issues creating the poor feedback. • To support the individual to shift the perception of their leadership style. • To increase satisfaction and engagement survey results. • To retain key members of the team.	**Coaching** by an external seems to fit most directly as: • the manager probably needs support within a structured process, e.g. one that is reviewed by HR • there is a need to target specific skills, e.g. communication, delegation • maintaining openness, trust and an objective/impartial viewpoint is essential and most easily indicated by use of an external coach.

A fairly confident Sales Manager is struggling to present effectively to groups – talks in too much detail, overruns, etc. Investigation shows a lack of awareness, e.g. the principles of presenting effectively.	• To have the Sales Manager operate from principles of effective presentations. • To increase the impact and efficiency of these sessions. • To improve both the perception of the board and the success of the individual.	Appears to be most directly related to a **training** need. For example: • The individual has a knowledge gap, e.g. presentation principles. • They would probably benefit from a 'shared' learning experience, i.e. with a group of people who also need to learn. • Once the individual has the knowledge, they can begin using it, after which the need can be reassessed.
A new hire is appointed as the fourth Finance Director (FD) in 20 months after the previous FD quit suddenly. The role has internally become known as 'the poison chalice' to indicate the difficult nature of the role and complex reporting lines and organisational structure.	• To avoid the financial risks created by frequent turnover of staff in this role. • To support the individual to be successful, e.g. reduce the pressure upon them. • To shift poor perception of the role, both internally and externally.	A **consultancy**-type intervention appears most likely as a first step where: • the role appears to have difficulties relating to structure and process, rather than people • by engaging services of an external specialist it communicates a clear intention to create change (to the rest of the organisation) • the situation appears to demand structured analysis, e.g. Is the organisational structure supporting someone to be effective?

▶

Situation	Requirements/ Objectives	Recommendation
A newly qualified teacher (NQT) has just joined a large, inner-city secondary school where the normal challenges of teaching 11–16 year olds are increased by issues of a broad range of ethnic backgrounds, religion and cultures.	• To support the NQT as they transition into a full-time teaching role, e.g. deal with day-to-day issues as they happen and learn principles to help guide them in situations. • To benefit from the wisdom and insight of someone with much greater experience of the distinct challenges of that particular school.	There appears a clear need for **mentoring**, when: • the individual doesn't need further theory (they have just qualified) so training seems less relevant • the individual has less practical knowledge or awareness to draw upon (and needs to access and develop that quickly) • they will benefit from having a one-to-one relationship of personal support during what might be a tough or challenging period.

Merge theory with your own experience

By now you'll notice some attributes of mentoring are simple to distinguish, for instance it's a one-on-one relationship focused on the development needs of a less-experienced person. You'll also notice that other principles are less clear-cut, e.g. 'What does 'help' mean in the context of a mentor relationship?' or 'How involved should I be in a mentee's situations?'

As we continue I will encourage you to use principles to consider these questions in combination with your situations. For example, you might decide that for your mentee, some types of 'helping' are appropriate, such as giving them a book on how to do well at job interviews. However, when you consider the principle that they need to learn to act for themselves, you might decide that other types of 'help' are inappropriate, e.g. offering to help write their CV for them. I'll be offering principles for you to combine with your own situations and experience to help you stay clear as to what's right for you as a mentor.

Chapter summary

Mentoring is a distinct relationship where one person (the mentor) supports the learning, development and progress of another person (the mentee). The mentor gives support by providing information, advice and assistance in a way that empowers the mentee. An effective mentor is able to stay flexible to the needs of the mentee in order to offer the appropriate types of assistance in a particular situation. For example, sometimes they are required to be a 'wise guide' and draw upon their own experiences to offer insight gained from their own journey. Sometimes the mentor adopts a more detached posture to act as a facilitator who helps the mentee to think and decide for themselves.

The mentor is engaged in the potential of the mentee to progress and be successful, and will often feel a sense of benevolence towards them. However, the mentor's role must remain unattached to a specific agenda or results, as ultimate responsibility for learning, progress and outcomes rests with the mentee.

2

Chapter

Jung viewed Freud as a mentor, but he never wanted to be anybody's disciple.

Viggo Mortensen, actor

What's different about a mentoring relationship?

In this chapter:

- Look at the distinct nature of the relationship a mentor has with the individual they are working with.
- Examine three typical themes that underpin all mentor relationships:
    - the 'quest' involving challenges which must be overcome
    - that the mentor has something the mentee needs
    - a harmony of benevolence and respect.
- Reflect on your existing knowledge and experience of these themes.

What's distinct about a mentor relationship?

To help us explore this idea further, let's remind ourselves of some classic mentor relationships – see Table 2.1 overleaf.

What can we use from this?

When we consider typical features of archetypal mentor relationships, the following themes appear consistently.

Table 2.1 Classic mentor relationships

Relationship	What the mentee seeks/ wants	What the mentor wants for the mentee	Attributes of the relationship
Professor Dumbledore: mentor to Harry Potter	Harry wants to defeat Voldemort and avenge his parents' murder.	• To keep Harry safe. • To help him learn and succeed (without interfering too much).	• Harry is respectful of Professor Dumbledore's position, status and reputation and so initially a little fearful too. • Dumbledore's sense of duty and his responsibility towards Harry are both personal and professional in nature.
Saul Berenson: mentor to Carrie Mathison (*Homeland*)	Carrie wants to be successful in defeating terrorist forces and ultimately to find true happiness.	• To encourage her to act both safely and appropriately in situations. • To assist her personal and professional success.	• Saul has experience and wisdom that Carrie needs. Saul and Carrie are united by friendship, mutual respect and trust. They are able to strongly disagree with each other, while maintaining commitment to the relationship.
Morpheus: mentor to Neo (*The Matrix*)	Neo's quest is to free the human race from the control of the matrix.	• To keep Neo alive. • To assist in his quest without inappropriate interference. To discover if Neo is 'the one'	• Morpheus appears to have wisdom and integrity and Neo chooses to trust Morpheus soon after meeting him. • Morpheus is initially doubting of Neo's potential but becomes more committed to him over time.
Ser Jorah Mormont to Daenerys Targaryen (*Game of Thrones*)	To reclaim her family's sovereignty over the seven kingdoms.	• To keep her safe and help her succeed.	• Ser Jorah believes in Daenerys and so takes an oath to serve and protect her. He consequently puts her interests before his own. • Daenerys has respect for Jorah's experience and knowledge, yet will ignore it when her intuition is strong.

Theme One: A journey or 'quest' involving challenges which must be overcome

From classic story-telling principles, a quest suggests a journey in search of something, or to achieve something that is truly valued. A quest also suggests 'a road of trials' or challenges and 'tests' to be overcome. As an extreme example, consider Jason and the Argonauts in the search for the Golden Fleece: they tackled screeching Harpies, skeleton warriors and a many-headed serpent known as Hydra along the way. Jason succeeded in his quest through a mix of courage, cunning and assistance from others. Other examples include *Lord of the Rings*, *The Hunger Games* and many role-play computer games.

While the examples are fantasy, they can easily be linked to our everyday experiences. Consider an important/valuable goal you have succeeded with in the past. Which of the following did it include?

- focused effort/energy on your part, e.g. perseverance, learning and/or hard work
- the need to overcome personal challenges, obstacles or false barriers, e.g. fear of failure, lack of ability/connections, inappropriate position, education or background
- the goodwill or practical assistance of others, e.g. from sponsors, friends and even complete strangers.

A temporary travelling companion

In stories, a mentor character often assists with a distinct adventure or quest, during which the person they are mentoring must triumph. In order to triumph, that person must overcome challenges and, through doing so, they emerge as strengthened and changed for the better. Since the idea of a journey easily translates to the on-going experience of life, where each of us is challenged by circumstances and events, the idea of a mentor playing a productive role for part of that journey is useful.

There is no education like adversity.

Benjamin Disraeli

If you imagine training for and running a marathon, then you probably start that expecting to encounter highs, lows and difficulties or obstacles that you must overcome. That might mean battling with your lack of fitness, poor eating habits, courage to keep going or simply the weather as you try to train and then run on the day. A mentor's function during your journey is to provide appropriate forms of assistance to help you succeed.

The mentee's desire sustains travel and provides focus

As a mentor, you can be more effective when the person you mentor wants something, perhaps to reach a destination or achieve something that is valuable to them. Without this sense of direction, the quality of your conversations may range from 'interesting discussion' to 'aimless chatter', both of which are unfulfilling for both parties in the long run.

Your mentee's goals might be to get better at something, such as managing people or handling pressure, or to secure promotion at work. They may also include intentions rather than clear goals, such as a desire to be a better leader or become more strategic in their outlook. These goals or intentions will require the individual to tackle challenges, overcome barriers or change their perspective, beliefs or mind-set. For example, the individual may need to learn to take personal risks in order to make change happen. Alternatively, they may need to take fewer risks in order to stop disasters happening. Everyone's journey is individual and the mentor works best when they stay aware of the unique nature of someone's quest.

Theme Two: The mentor has something the mentee needs

A core function of your role as a mentor is to provide an appropriate type of assistance to the mentee in a way that helps them reach their desired outcome, such as gaining a certain role or more time to spend with family. As a mentor, your assistance can take various forms, from the tangible to the intangible. For example, you might have:

- specific experience, knowledge or wisdom on a topic, e.g. mergers, leading people, managing through organisational change
- status or position that the mentee might benefit from, e.g. by understanding your world view, or gaining your unique perspectives
- contacts or a network that you are willing to share, e.g. 'I'll introduce you to someone who might be good for you to know'
- personal qualities or attributes that the mentee can learn and develop from, e.g. entrepreneurial spirit, tenacity or ability to create change through people
- specific skills that the mentee needs to learn, e.g. financial analysis and reporting, risk management, industry regulation.

As a mentor, your assistance can take various forms, from the tangible to the intangible

Story Teller

The assistance a mentee imagines they need, and the assistance they actually need, are often different.

Frustrated by what he felt was a stagnating career, Simon wanted a senior mentor to help smooth his career path by making appropriate introductions and recommendations on his behalf.

Simon was assigned a mentor called Judy. Judy was a department manager – two levels below the seniority Simon had hoped for, which initially disappointed him. Judy was also less interested in quick career success and more focused on taking roles that she found an enjoyable challenge and which offered experiences that would develop her professionally and personally.

▶

Judy's last two job moves had been sideways rather than upwards, to give her greater exposure to different areas of the business.

Judy's logic was that by gaining a broad experience earlier in her career she would gain benefits later as she rose to more senior levels. For example, by truly understanding how the business operated and gaining a variety of contacts and skills, she would become an automatic choice for an executive role over time.

Through his mentoring conversations with Judy, Simon came to imagine his career as a pyramid of building blocks or stages, each stacking upon the other, where the most valuable blocks were the broad foundation stones that created a solid base upon which to build. He realised that winning a senior executive role was one thing, and being successful at it over time was another.

Judy may not have been the mentor Simon had wanted, but she turned out to have just the experience and perspective that he learned to value over time. While that may sound convenient, or coincidental, it is a perspective that is available to all mentees, i.e. that we always get the mentor we need (and not necessarily the mentor we want).

What does 'appropriate assistance' mean?

We discussed earlier that the mentor's function is to provide 'appropriate assistance' in support of the mentee's progress towards a desired future or goal. To decide what assistance is appropriate requires you to combine logic, wisdom and intuition. This is a challenge that runs through both your individual conversations and the overall relationship. As a mentor there are many forms of assistance that you might provide. Here are just a few:

• Share experience, e.g. tell stories and offer your views on topics that the mentee is interested in.

- Provide space for the mentee to think things through, e.g. 'So what's really important about this?' or 'What causes that?' or 'So what are your realistic options?'

- Offer constructive feedback, e.g. 'You appear to be procrastinating a little over this' or 'I think you don't set clear boundaries for people.'

- Give advice or wise counsel, e.g. 'I think if you drive the team too hard on delivery you risk losing their support in the longer term' or 'Your greatest form of influence is relationships – work on building those first.'

- Share your knowledge, e.g. 'Let me explain how the reporting works across a typical project of this size' or 'There are regulations in force designed to stop that being possible.'

- Share power or influence, e.g. 'I can get you invited to that' or 'Tell HR I recommended you for the event.'

- Share your network of contacts, e.g. 'It would be good for you to meet Ewan – let me introduce you' or 'Here are the names of people who are the most influential in that community.'

How do you decide what 'appropriate assistance' is?

Most of us develop our ability to mentor through experience, trial and error, and learning from what worked and what didn't. Even if you are given initial training to be a mentor, ultimately you will learn the most through practice. So this question of 'appropriate assistance' is one that you need to consider regularly to maintain effectiveness. In the absence of clear-cut rules as to what type of assistance to provide in which circumstances, as a mentor your considerations include:

- What principles have you agreed during the beginning stages of the mentoring assignment, e.g. the type of help your mentee is hoping for, the type of support you want to offer, plus any organisational guidelines?

- How clear or strong is your view of the situation, e.g. are you convinced about what needs to happen, or what your mentee should do?

- What are the features of the immediate situation, e.g. how much time pressure does the mentee face to make progress? What are the risks involved in the situation? How important is it? (Perhaps they will benefit more from potentially making mistakes.)

- What approach will most benefit the mentee's learning and progress? Might you tell stories as a gentle way of offering ideas and thoughts or might the point you want to make get lost?

- What are you willing to do? For example, giving advice can be easier than facilitating your mentee's thoughts using questioning and listening. Or you may have reservations about sharing contacts or making introductions if you feel your mentee may not respect/value those appropriately.

Even if you are given initial training to be a mentor, ultimately you will learn the most through practice

The best approach is ultimately determined by results

While there is no right or wrong in the type of assistance that you offer, there are 'better' and 'worse' types of assistance which are determined by the results they create. For example, you may take an easier route of story telling because you enjoy talking about yourself and it's something you are comfortable doing. But if the mentee doesn't benefit in some way from hearing your stories, then telling them was an ineffective form of assistance. Perhaps a mixture of stories and facilitation might work better, e.g. 'What are you most interested in hearing about?' or 'What similarities do you see between your situation and my own?'

Theme Three: A harmony of benevolence and respect

Effective mentor relationships are fuelled by a reciprocal blend of benevolence and respect. The quality of benevolence comes from you (the mentor) towards your mentee, while the quality of respect comes from your mentee towards you. It's possible that both qualities are mutual; that you also respect your mentee, or your mentee also feels benevolent towards you. However, these features are less important in driving the effectiveness of the relationship.

The qualities of benevolence and respect can be seen most obviously in the more traditional role of an experienced, wise and older person mentoring a younger, less-experienced person. It's easy to imagine that someone towards the end of their career (or life) would feel benevolent towards someone younger than themselves, perhaps as a way of 'giving something back'. It's also natural for someone young and aspirational to respect an older person who has been successful in some way that is relevant to them, such as in building a business or achieving career success. However, for modern-day mentoring we are able to detach the factor of age from the qualities of benevolence and respect. In organisations especially, mentoring regularly happens where a large age gap is less relevant than attributes such as life experience, mind-set or world view. These qualities of benevolence and respect are relevant regardless of age, simply because of the nature of the relationship they help to develop.

The significance of benevolence

One feature that helps to distinguish mentoring from activities such as coaching, consultancy or management is that the mentor has some level of benevolence towards the mentee. By benevolence I mean a sense of goodwill towards the mentee or the qualities of compassion, care and generosity. As a mentor these qualities help you to create a personal sense of commitment towards the person you are mentoring.

The levels of compassion, care and generosity a mentor feels will vary from relationship to relationship and need to stay within boundaries of professionalism and effectiveness. Indeed, while we may feel a personal sense of commitment towards our mentee's progress, we often need to stay uninvolved in the mentee's affairs. Reasons for this include:

- Your mentee needs to feel ownership for their own learning.
- Your mentee must not be protected from life's formative/ tougher lessons, e.g. how to cope with disappointment, pressure or fear.
- Your mentee is empowered when they are successful through their own efforts.

For example, using the above principles, perhaps you really want your mentee to succeed in a job interview and are willing to meet for an extra session or two to help them rehearse. That's fine. What is less appropriate is that you phone your mentee repeatedly through the interview stages, or become involved in the process, e.g. by volunteering a biased/overly positive reference to the hiring manager.

The principle of benevolence will help sustain your commitment and flexibility towards your mentee, while not suggesting responsibility for them.

What if the mentor doesn't feel benevolent?

If, as a mentor, you don't feel benevolent or compassionate towards your mentee, it does not mean that you are unable to work with the mentee in a way that is helpful. After all, you can still share knowledge, give advice, etc. This type of mentoring is more 'transactional' in nature in that it functions on an exchange of ideas and information in a series of mutually convenient conversations. There is nothing wrong with a 'transactional approach' to the relationship; however, the lack of benevolence does change the nature of your relationship. For example, where benevolence is lacking, you potentially increase your sense of detachment towards the mentee. While doing that isn't necessarily a 'bad' thing, you are potentially increasing intolerance or decreasing your commitment, e.g. 'I appreciate the situation but I'm still not willing to do a call after hours.'

Increased detachment reduces the personal tone of the relationship and that personal tone can be of great value to the mentee. When the mentee recognises warmth and compassion from you, they are likely to benefit from that. For example, they are likely to feel safer in conversation, less 'judged' and more supported. This enables them to disclose their thoughts more openly and perhaps tackle tougher/previously concealed issues.

The mentee has respect for the mentor

Part of your skill as an effective mentor is to maintain a sense of respect from your mentee. This is because when we respect someone we are more open to learning from them, and to being influenced by them. The respect that a mentee has for their mentor might be easily/quickly given, for instance because of the mentor's profile or position. It may also be reluctant respect, e.g. 'I don't like him/her but I respect what they do.' Quite often this quality of respect grows over time, e.g. 'I now see why they are a great mentor for me.' What is important is that ultimately your mentee regards you as someone they can learn from or be supported by in some way.

Part of your skill as an effective mentor is to maintain a sense of respect from your mentee

How do you encourage and maintain respect?

While respect is sometimes given easily, it is more often earned – for example, when we consistently display qualities that our mentee values in some way, such as wisdom, integrity or strength of character. What creates respect in an individual is as unique as they are and links to what they value, fear or aspire to. For example, if you fear and avoid giving presentations to large audiences, you might respect someone who overcame their own fear to do that. Or if you struggle to stay fit and eat healthily, you might respect someone who regularly runs marathons. As you give your respect to that person, you open yourself to be both influenced and inspired by them. As they share what has been possible for them, they may be pointing to what is also possible for you.

What if the mentee doesn't respect the mentor?

If the mentee lacks respect for the mentor, it may range from a temporary issue to a clear source of problem. For example, perhaps early on the mentee is unclear as to the value of the individual assigned to them and simply needs to get to know them further and continue with the mentoring conversations. This 'lack of respect' is passive and more an absence of something that will grow naturally over time. However, in a different situation the mentee's lack of respect may deteriorate into the opposite of respect: contempt. Contempt is not passive but an active sense that the other person is undeserving of respect and more deserving of criticism. While extreme contempt is rare, even a mild form may result in the following types of responses from a mentee:

- showing up late or cancelling meetings at short notice
- displaying a lack of listening, e.g. frequently interrupting or constantly disagreeing
- consistently ignoring the advice or opinion of the mentor
- displaying little respect for the mentoring process, e.g. 'I'm getting nothing from this' or 'It's a waste of time'
- criticism of the mentor, e.g. 'He/she does not impress me/has nothing to offer me.'

The above list makes for uncomfortable reading, and it's useful to acknowledge that these behaviours may be unrelated to anything the mentor has actually done. We choose how we see the world, what we value and what we don't. Put simply, sometimes as a mentor, we can't actually win because the mentee has decided to be disappointed early on in the relationship. Perhaps they have been assigned a man and wanted a woman, or someone with a certain role, status, etc. Ironically, as a mentor, any 'over-efforting' on your part to earn respect of the mentee can actually create contempt. To avoid creating a problem, you are wise to operate from a principle of assuming that you have respect until you know that you don't.

One of the most sincere forms of respect is actually listening to what another has to say.

Bryant H. McGill

Checklist

Behaviours that help build respect from others

Display professionalism and self-discipline: arrive for meetings on time, encourage the meetings to end on time and complete the conversation effectively.

✔ Encourage the mentee's interest, e.g. by sharing your achievements, interests and values.

✔ Be authentic or 'real' for them, by acting naturally, disclosing mistakes or limits where appropriate, etc.

✔ Demonstrate integrity by aligning your behaviours with your advice (rather than simply giving advice/ principles that you yourself don't follow).

✔ Demonstrate respect for the mentee, e.g. showing interest in them and what's important to them, listening to them, displaying an ability to retain information about them, etc.

Chapter summary

The nature of the relationship between a mentor and a mentee distinguishes the activity from any other form of learning and development support. In addition, the quality of that relationship directly impacts the potential success of the mentoring activity, i.e. the progress that the mentee is able to make by being mentored. Mentoring relationships can be indicated by three consistent themes:

1. A journey or 'quest' involving challenges which must be overcome.

2. That the mentor has something the mentee needs.

3. A harmony of benevolence and respect.

As a mentor, it is important that you understand your mentee's vision and aspirations and consider what assistance is appropriate to offer them. You must also decide how personally committed you are comfortable being while maintaining proper boundaries of involvement. Finally, you need to build and maintain the respect of the mentee if you are to be able to influence them constructively.

Chapter 3

There are many paths but only one journey.

Naomi Judd, singer-songwriter

Guiding principles for mentors

In this chapter:

- Learn principles that will help guide your actions as a mentor.
- Learn to balance your commitment to someone's progress with an appropriate sense of detachment.
- Gain points of future reference that you can return to, i.e. as you begin to mentor others.

The following principles are intended to guide and test your thinking, e.g. 'This has happened, what should I do?' Some of the principles will feel logical and like 'common sense' while others ask that you reflect a little, to decide whether or not you agree with the principle and wish to adopt it for yourself. The principles I encourage you to adopt are:

1. Your relationship is one of equality and yet has a natural bias/emphasis.
2. The responsibility for learning, progress and results ultimately rests with your mentee.
3. Mentoring is collaboration between you, your mentee and 'everyday life'.
4. Ultimately, what your mentee chooses to do, learn or ignore from the mentoring is not the mentor's business.
5. Some results of mentoring can be identified or measured, while some results cannot. (This does not mean they are insignificant or less important, it simply means you are less aware of them.)

Let's look at each principle a little more closely.

1. The relationship is one of equality and yet has a natural bias/emphasis

A meeting of equals

From your perspective as a mentor, the relationship is a meeting of equals, even though you might often be judged more 'senior' than the person you are mentoring. In an organisational context especially, it's a natural feature that someone more experienced might have a more senior role, or be considered to have more status in the relationship. It's true that there is a need to acknowledge and focus upon this; for example, what you have learned through experience may have contributed to your situation or success. This creates a natural emphasis or bias towards what you think and believe as a mentor. Where your intention as mentor is to provide support and guidance to assist your mentee's progress, it is natural that you draw upon your experience and learning to do this.

A need for empowerment

However, it's also necessary for the collaboration to 'work' in relationship terms. This means that the mentee should feel at ease to discuss potentially difficult or awkward topics, ask tough questions and get to grips with the realities of your experience. Where a mentee is overly daunted by the status or demeanour of their mentor, conversations are likely to remain polite and potentially constrained in content. Another pitfall when we wield too much power in the conversation is that we might assume we are 'managing' the mentee, perhaps through making requests of them, giving instructions, 'homework', etc.

Leadership is not defined by the exercise of power but by the ability to increase the sense of power among those who are led.

Mary Parker Follett

The mentor's aim is to support the mentee's growth and progress while increasing their sense of empowerment; if the mentor tries to 'manage' them, this is clearly counterproductive. In Mary Parker Follett's quote, her wisdom translates to the true power of mentoring, not simply of leadership. For example, while a mentee may value the clarity they experience by being given instructions, they may also become dependent on the directive style of their mentor. Ending the relationship may then prove detrimental, perhaps because the mentee's confidence to act is now dependent on the direction of their mentor. Alternatively, they have followed the mentor's requests and maintained their confidence, but have not understood the principles the mentor was using and so cannot continue with the same clarity independently.

The mentor's aim is to support the mentee's growth and progress while increasing their sense of empowerment

It's like a manager responding to two identical emailed requests from two different team members. Both team members ask for a day's leave at short notice. With the first person the manager may refuse the request and ask them to come and discuss the situation, while with the second person they may send a simple response of 'Yes, of course'. Without understanding the principles the manager operates from to make their decisions, someone else cannot demonstrate the same wisdom.

2. Responsibility for learning, progress and results ultimately rests with the mentee

This principle places the responsibility for learning and growth with the mentee. It means that if the mentee is not making progress or meeting their objectives for the sessions, then it is the mentee who has the primary duty to act. When you work on this principle throughout the mentoring relationship, it enables both parties to retain a healthy perspective on situations. It stems from the following needs:

- to place the ownership of the mentee's results where they belong (with the mentee)
- to encourage the mentee to feel empowered in their circumstances, i.e. 'I can do this'
- to help the mentee build commitment, e.g. 'I'll get out of this what I put into it'
- for the mentor to avoid 'interfering' from a sense of personal agenda or desire to rescue, e.g. 'They aren't getting this, so I need to step in and fix the situation'
- for the mentor to retain a healthy perspective, e.g. 'I'm committed to their growth and progress but not attached to that.'

Where there might be a natural tendency for us to want to 'help' or encourage success for the mentee, the potential to feel some ownership or begin to have a specific agenda for the mentee's progress increases. For example, we may feel that the mentee is more interested in discussing their problems than solving them and that the mentee 'needs to learn to take positive action'. This may be valid and useful feedback for us to offer. However, if we allow ourselves to become frustrated about the apparent inaction, or begin to make offers to get more involved in situations, then the balance of the relationship might shift. This idea of having a 'personal agenda' for a mentee is covered further in Chapter 6.

What you evaluate ... you emphasise

Where a mentor is evaluated as part of a mentoring scheme, perhaps to understand their approach or spot issues such as mismatched relationships, we can easily start to feel a sense of pressure to create 'results', i.e. for our mentee to be suddenly suc-cessful, or to 'change' in some way. While there might be benefit in evaluating a mentor's style of approach, or even behavioural skills, it is less relevant to judge a mentor on what the mentee is doing as a result of the conversations.

Checklist

How do you know you are an effective mentor?

1 Your handling of the process

✔ Do you keep your agreements, e.g. arrive for sessions on time, send information as promised, etc.?

✔ Do you appear engaged in the process, e.g. appear positive and optimistic in relation to the sessions, or do you appear unenthusiastic, often cancel at the last minute, etc.?

✔ Do you appear committed to the mentee's progress, e.g. demonstrate interest in them and their challenges, share personal learning and insight, etc.?

2 Your approach

✔ Do you share appropriate personal and professional information in support of the mentee's progress and learning?

✔ Do you demonstrate an understanding of the operating principles of mentoring, e.g. encourage the mentee to retain responsibility for their learning?

✔ Do you focus on barriers and blocks in order to help the mentee remove them?

3 Your behavioural skill

✔ Do you build rapport easily, i.e. do you put the mentee at their ease, promote openness and trust?

✔ Do you bring appropriate levels of challenge to conversations, e.g. observations, opinions and constructive feedback?

✔ Do you facilitate the mentee's thinking processes, e.g. through effective listening, offering summaries, asking open questions, etc.?

Start as you intend to continue

The principle of responsibility for learning and progress resting with the mentee works best when agreed up front as part of orientation: when you and your mentee agree how you want to work together. If the relationship happens within the context of a mentoring scheme, this principle can be explained in set-up information, when the mentee is given an overview of what mentoring is, what it isn't, etc.

3. Mentoring is a collaboration between you, your mentee and 'everyday life'

This is a more philosophical principle to help you, the mentor, relax and trust the overall process of which you are a part. The principle is that mentoring is collaboration between you, your mentee and everyday life, with all of its unexpected developments and events. As a mentor, you can make an effort to increase certainty in a relationship, e.g. build on a firm footing of objectives, agreements and expectations, work to stay focused and aligned, etc. Yet ultimately it is not possible to predict what will happen once sessions have begun, e.g. how events might appear to conspire for/against the progress of the assignment.

Did you ever think a situation would turn out a certain way and it didn't? Or have you ever thought you knew someone but then they did something that was unexpected? A mentor relationship may begin in one direction and switch to another: perhaps you thought you were helping someone to gain promotion, then they decide they want to reduce the pressure on themselves by finding a simpler role. Ultimately, your mentee and their on-going circumstances are beyond your ability to know fully or predict with certainty.

A mentor relationship may begin in one direction and switch to another

Embrace the unexpected and reduce your resistance to it

Where we are unable to control life's twists and turns, it is more logical to accept them and even embrace them. By 'embrace them' I mean that we accept that all events are ideal from a 'big picture' perspective, even if we may never be able to see from that viewpoint. It's like deciding to believe that it was ideal that you were turned down by a potential employer or even a potential life partner because in the overall scenario there was a benefit to that. Sometimes we are fortunate to see the benefit, e.g. you got a job/partner more suited to you, and sometimes we don't see it.

> *And whether or not it is clear to you, no doubt the universe is unfolding as it should.*
>
> Max Ehrmann

The purpose of taking on this belief is not because we can prove it is true but simply because there are benefits to doing so, such as the following:

- By embracing a situation we are able to stay resourceful and constructive as our emotional resistance to a situation is lessened, e.g. 'I can't believe I didn't get the job!' shifts to 'okay, so I didn't get the job – now what?'
- When we accept a situation, we can decide what the most resourceful response is to that situation, e.g. 'If I'm not right for them, maybe they're not right for me' or 'I need to learn from this and begin again.'
- We encourage a sense of being enriched by all situations and events, e.g. 'I'm now much stronger/wiser', etc.
- Over time, we develop a sense of trust that can pervade all our situations. This enables us to feel less concern or doubt about our overall well-being and ability to prevail.
- To believe the opposite may lead us into a spiral of negativity, e.g. 'Life's against me, so what's the point?'

To place the idea in the context of your mentoring, here are some potential 'twists and turns' to illustrate:

- Your mentee arrives late for a session and then explains they need to leave 30 minutes early.
- Your meeting room is double booked and you don't have anywhere to meet.
- The mentee shows up without their notes from the last session and appears totally unprepared for this one.
- Your mentee moves work location and you can no longer meet face to face.
- Your mentee requests more frequent and longer sessions but you know you cannot accommodate the additional investment of time.
- In the last session your mentee complained about their 'impossible' workload and they arrive for this session to explain it just got bigger.
- HR contacts you to explain that your mentee wants to finish the sessions because they don't feel they are getting enough value from them to justify the investment of time.

I'm sure you have your own versions of the above – unexpected developments that you can respond to resourcefully – or not! It might be a minor, unexpected event or a major change of circumstances. Within mentoring, we go one step further, in that we need to see everything that happens as an ideal stage along the journey. Again, as we reduce resistance, we increase acceptance, which helps us stay constructive. We are also embracing the concept of 'the road of trials' (or useful challenges from which the mentee can learn and grow), which shaped our first theme of the relationship in Chapter 2.

> *A gem cannot be polished without friction, nor a man perfected without trials.*
>
> Lucius Annaeus Seneca

Embrace does not mean 'become victim to'

This principle of 'embracing' what happens within a mentoring assignment is not to make you passive or 'victim' to it but more to enable you to maintain an objective viewpoint that is resilient in response to life's twists and turns.

> *Resilience is all about being able to overcome the unexpected. The goal of resilience is to thrive.*
>
> Jamais Cascio

Accepting and embracing something does not mean that we don't try to change things, just that we don't waste emotional energy resisting 'what is'. This then frees up our energy to focus on a more resourceful response.

Let's use the example where your mentee moves work location, which requires you to work together differently (have telephone calls, Skype/video-conference sessions, use email, etc.) to see how the principle might impact your thinking.

- My mentee is moving location and that means we can't meet face to face any more.
    - How can I see that as ideal, e.g. something ultimately constructive?
    - What options have now become available? (To do something differently, change approach, etc.)
    - What might the benefits of this be?

Table 3.1 shows how the principle plays out over time, compared with a more resistant approach.

Table 3.1 The principle of 'embracing'

Response from frustration and resistance	Response from 'accept and embrace'
Short term: • You feel disappointed and potentially frustrated. • You consider the risks of not having face-to-face sessions, e.g. reduced personal connection, rapport, etc. • You look for options that reduce the loss of the face-to-face sessions.	**Short term:** • You register the development with interest. • You wonder how this might be perfect, e.g. 'I wonder how this is going to benefit the mentee over time?' • You work creatively to understand options, e.g. 'What different things could we try doing to support their progress?'
Long term: • You view the new approach to sessions as a compromise, which might impact your attitude or mood during sessions. • You maintain a sense of 'this is not ideal', at least until you gain clear evidence to the contrary. • Your perception of the relationship shifts – you might become a little more detached or 'remote'.	**Long term:** • You continue with the mentoring sessions with complete acceptance of the changed circumstances. • You remain interested to discover how working together in new ways, e.g. via Skype, transpires as beneficial for the situation. • You continue to feel 'freed up' to mentor the individual.

By embracing what happens during an assignment, we develop a perspective or 'filter' that enables us to view the positives in a situation. Here are just a few of the ways this development might show itself to be a constructive event in the mentee's journey.

• You both agree to Skype and that requires better preparation and organisation to be effective. This quality is something that the mentee has previously lacked and so they are now being presented with the choice to add effort to make the mentoring assignment work, or not.

- It's a useful dilemma that highlights a need for them to decide how committed to the mentoring they actually are.

- They learn how to become effective during remote meetings, i.e. Skype, video conferencing, telephone, etc. That proves a valuable skill for them generally (as it is a more frequent element of their role).

What about the impact on the mentor?

As a mentor you might be wondering, 'So what about the impact or inconvenience to me?' and of course the answer is: the relationship isn't about you, it's about your mentee. Remember, the primary purpose of the relationship is to benefit the learning and progress of the mentee. This doesn't mean that the mentor should suffer (the relationship is one of equals), but simply that your focus is mainly on the mentee.

4. Ultimately, what the mentee chooses to do, learn or ignore from the mentoring is not the mentor's business

This is another philosophical principle to help you remain resourceful and resilient as a mentor. Where an effective mentor is engaged in the opportunity to help their mentee learn, develop and progress, there can be a tendency to become emotionally invested in a certain outcome for them. It might be that you want your mentee to make what you believe are better choices, or to change certain behaviours or tendencies. Perhaps your mentee tells you about an opportunity to go for an internal job interview, which you feel would be a hugely positive experience, but then they decide against it, saying that they 'don't feel ready' either for the interview process or for the change involved if they were offered a new, more senior role. You notice that they have a tendency to avoid situations that make them anxious (such as job interviews) and that appears to be what's holding them back from attaining the career success they say they want. You give them that feedback and their response indicates they accept your view, e.g. 'Maybe you're right, but I just don't feel comfortable at the idea of this.'

Imagine, then, that you convince them to go for the job interview. The experience might turn out in a number of ways:

1. They are successful at the interview and they thank you for encouraging them to go for it. They excel in their new role.

2. Their fear of interviews is embedded – they 'froze' several times, resulting in a 'failure' type of experience for them and a negative impression with the interviewers.

3. They are successful in interview and are offered the job, but then refuse it as they follow their instinct that they 'aren't ready' – again creating a poor impression with the interviewers.

4. They are successful, accept the job but are not able to tackle its challenges and pressure, and so move jobs fairly soon afterwards.

5. They are offered the position, begin the new role and then when a different role that they want much more is advertised shortly afterwards, they are unable to apply for it.

The purpose of this list is simply to acknowledge the many different ways that events can develop, and that on-going consequences are unseen to us in the present moment.

Remain interested in what your mentee does – and not invested in it

This principle that 'what they do is ultimately not your business' is not intended to dissuade you from being interested in what your mentee does. The principle simply means that the extent of your involvement ('your business') is to offer, to advise, to support, to facilitate, to help, to guide – and that's all. So this principle can provide a helpful boundary for you, which will help you to relax about what happens outside of your mentoring conversations (as something beyond your control). That's why what someone chooses to do or not do is 'not your business'. A little like a bookshop owner's 'business' is to offer then sell books to people, not to make sure they read them from cover to cover.

By adopting this principle, you are remaining impartial to potential outcomes. This doesn't mean you are not interested in what your mentee does – of course you will be! I encourage you to demonstrate interest – ask them what they've been doing, listen as they tell you, retain key information, etc. This also doesn't mean to say that you don't care about what happens, merely that you will retain a balanced view of it. If you accept that empowering someone else is more valuable than fixing things for them, then this principle is logical and hopefully acceptable to you.

Notice the influence of your ego

If we are motivated to experience the pleasure of what we see as a successful outcome or the gratification of the mentee 'getting it right', then when their actions fall short of our expectations, we may feel frustrated. This is often because we are being influenced by our ego. Our ego is a function of our mind and creates our sense of 'who we are', such as 'I am a daughter, husband, manager, mentor, etc.'. Some of the functions of the ego are practical, as when it judges and compares in a helpful way the difference between ourselves and the world around us. Other functions are less helpful, perhaps born from a need to sustain our sense of 'who we are'. For example, perhaps some of the following statements might resonate as true for you:

- I need to maintain a sense of control in situations.
- I need to stay in a feeling of the 'known' and avoid a feeling of being in the 'unknown', e.g. 'I'm more comfortable talking about what I know about.'
- I am gratified by receiving approval from others.
- I need to maintain a sense of being 'right' in situations and so avoid being proved wrong.
- I need to feel approved of (liked/loved) and therefore work to please or impress others.

Our ego is a function of our mind and creates our sense of 'who we are'

Among the fixations of the ego is a compulsion to 'know' or 'be certain'. Depending on the individual, this can express itself in a range of ways: from constant study (seeking to know), to refusing to learn, e.g. 'I know all I need to know!' As a mentor, it is important to consider your ego's (mind's) influence upon you as it may shape your behaviours and responses to some situations. For example, if the mentee asks you to explain how to understand a company's financial report and you don't know exactly how to do that, your responses may vary:

- You say that you don't know (and refer them to another source of information).
- You might use the little understanding you have to exaggerate your knowledge, e.g. ignore/skim over the elements you don't know and focus on those that you do.
- You might dismiss the question, e.g. 'You don't need to know that stuff, plus it's probably invented anyway.'

When you understand how your ego is affecting you, then you are more able to acknowledge and ignore the effect. This may incur some discomfort, as you also acknowledge and ignore a feeling of exposure in a situation. Using the previous example: as you realise 'I'm going to have to admit I don't actually know this', you might feel awkward because you imagine you look less impressive or even stupid. However, by ignoring your ego, you choose to be open about not knowing in order to maintain your sense of integrity, by telling the truth in the situation.

Let's try a quick test. When you first read the principle 'What the mentee does is not your business', did that bother you or perhaps even offend you in some way? If you did feel some level of discomfort with that, then your discomfort is probably your ego showing itself. If it didn't, try to think of another situation where you might have felt offended, e.g. perhaps someone criticised or ignored you and that made you feel affronted in some way. Again, your discomfort is caused as your ego (or your sense of self/who you are) feels vulnerable or exposed. Our ego likes to retain a perception of being superior in situations, because when we are superior, we are more 'safe'. The statement 'it's not your business' suggests that you are not superior (and so beyond reproach), which may make our ego squirm a little.*

To gain more awareness of your ego's influence upon you, try the following exercise.

Exercise

Approval or control?

Think of three situations you are currently frustrated or disappointed about – perhaps situations you view as problems, or events that made you unhappy in some way. Write those three items in a quick list. For example:

1 I presented for the senior team recently and didn't make a good impression. I'm disappointed at my performance and keep replaying it in my mind.

2 We thought we'd sold our property, but the buyers have just withdrawn their offer, which means we can't move after all.

3 My boss is really annoying me (he doesn't respond to my emails, cancels one-to-one meetings, etc.) and he's really blocking my progress in several areas.

Next, consider each issue in combination with the following question:

● In this situation, what are you making important: approval or control?

For each situation, it's most likely that you will be drawn by the idea that you need to maintain or gain approval in some way (most obvious in issue 1), or else you seek control of a situation and don't have that (most obvious in issue 2). In some situations, it may be a need for both approval and control, which is possibly present in issue 3.

* If you are interested to learn more about the ego and its impact upon your behaviours, you'll find further discussion in my book *Brilliant Coaching*. For fuller immersion in the subject, I recommend that you read *A New Earth* by Eckhart Tolle.

Next, reflect upon each of your three issues using the following question:

- What would giving up the need for control or approval do to this situation?

As you consider your situations and then relax a need for approval and/or control, you also lessen the influence of your ego upon your perspective. This can free up your mind to consider different responses or viewpoints. Again with the same situations, use the following questions to help you do this:

- When you give up a need for approval and/or control:
  - What fresh perspective or choices are now available?
  - How might you act differently?
  - What else would change?

The 'giving up' questions can help you relax the unconscious drivers of approval and control, and help you stay more impartial to a situation. As you mentor others, use these questions whenever you think they might help you move to a more objective position, e.g. if you are perhaps ever disappointed or frustrated with your mentee, the process or even yourself.

We'll cover the topic of the ego further in Chapter 6 as we explore the pitfalls of putting yourself under pressure and trying to maintain status in the relationship. For now, simply consider that some of what shapes your thinking and behaviour in situations is born from a basic need to maintain a positive appearance and retain a sense of control, or 'be in charge'. Those are natural human tendencies and not a problem in themselves; the potential issue occurs when the tendencies overrule what we know to be the 'right' or truthful or authentic response in a situation – such as sometimes admitting we are wrong, or don't know, or even that we need help. Remember, a mentor is made more accessible by their imperfections rather than any false façade of perfection.

A mentor is made more accessible by their imperfections

5. Some results of mentoring can be known or measured, and some results cannot

With any type of one-to-one intervention, there is a tendency to want impressive improvements, outcomes and results. Where the assignment forms part of a company-wide scheme, the organisation may especially want to evaluate results from the mentoring activity along criteria such as increased promotion rate of mentees, less talent lost to competitors, etc. In addition, the mentor might want to 'feel good' about the work that they are doing and seek confirmation through the mentee's achievements.

> *Not everything that counts can be counted, and not everything that can be counted counts.*
>
> William Bruce Cameron, author

While William Bruce Cameron's principle may appear philosophical, it is actually based in reality: what is ultimately beneficial to the learning and progress of a mentee may not reveal itself, whether within the timeframe of an assignment, in the conscious mind of a mentee, or as something directly linked to the mentoring sessions. Just because an impact or outcome of a mentoring assignment is less obvious or delayed does not mean that it is insignificant or less important; it simply means you are less aware of them. Here are some examples of that:

- The mentee grew to appreciate the mentor's calm demeanour over time as they experienced their mentor's tendency to reflect more objectively and deeply in order to arrive at considered conclusions and insights. As a result, they unconsciously picked up a tendency to emulate this style of response with colleagues, which in turn had a positive impact on the quality and outcomes of those conversations.

- The mentee was impressed by the mentor's refusal to accept challenges as 'problems' and they were particularly inspired by the mentor's response to an unexpected career setback. Years later, when the mentee experienced something similar, they were able to draw upon the principles they had watched their mentor use, e.g. 'accept and embrace every development as a perfect part of an unseen plan'.

- The mentee realised that the mentor had a much more professional appearance than they did, e.g. their manner of dress, the way they spoke succinctly and yet with impact, etc. As a result of this, the mentee smartened up their work clothes, reduced their tendency to ramble in conversations and generally polished their professional manner. Even though this had a significant positive effect, this was not something they were comfortable sharing with others, e.g. they would not disclose the benefit on an evaluation form.

The principle that some results can be measured and some can't is intended to strengthen your approach rather than dilute it. It means that you can stay committed to supporting your mentee to make progress and trust that you are doing that, even when you are sometimes unable to identify exactly how that progress is happening. Rather than becoming attached to 'quick results' or specific sequences of events, I encourage that you:

- use the principles of an effective mentor to help guide your decisions and behaviours
- maintain a focus on the key attributes and function of a mentor (these are covered in Chapter 4)
- adopt a little supporting structure from the basic process in Chapter 5.

When you develop consistency with the above, all that is left to do is trust that you will make a positive difference to whomever you support as a mentor. Sometimes the results you help to create stay unseen to you; sometimes they will show up unexpectedly to surprise and delight you. However, seeking to make certain results happen, or becoming overly concerned that you are not making a difference, does not help your confidence or your enjoyment as a mentor.

One cannot plan for the unexpected.

Aaron Klug, chemist and biophysicist

Chapter summary

Where the on-going activity of mentoring someone incorporates uncertainty and challenge, we need effective principles to help guide and sustain us along the way. Some principles are obvious and don't need discussing, e.g. an effective mentor is committed to the success of the mentee. However, some principles are less obvious as they are derived from more subtle dilemmas caused by our unconscious preferences. The principles that effective mentors adopt include:

1. Your relationship is one of equality and yet has a natural bias/emphasis.

2. The responsibility for learning, progress and results ultimately rests with your mentee.

3. Mentoring is collaboration between you, your mentee and 'everyday life'.

4. Ultimately, what your mentee chooses to do, learn or ignore from the mentoring is not the mentor's business.

5. Some results of mentoring can be identified or measured, while some results cannot. (This does not mean they are insignificant or less important, it simply means you are less aware of them.)

Staying aware of the above principles and reviewing them occasionally can help us maintain constructive views of situations and make resourceful choices in relation to them.

4

Chapter

Experience is not what happens to you; it's what
you do with what happens to you.

Aldous Huxley, author

What do good mentors do well?

In this chapter:

- Learn the common tendencies or abilities of great mentors.
- Compare your own tendencies in relation to these, e.g. 'Do I do this?'
- Accelerate your development as a mentor by deciding what ability you want to focus on.

What does it take to be a mentor?

In this chapter, we will look at common tendencies of great mentors, abilities they have that result in successful mentoring relationships. By using the word 'tendencies', I mean things that they typically do during an active mentor relationship. So these are less 'skills' in the usual sense of the term, such as asking great questions, giving feedback and building rapport. However, these skills (giving feedback, asking great questions, etc.) are still relevant for you to develop as they increase your effectiveness and impact generally, not just as a mentor.* The primary abilities that directly support successful mentoring relationships are:

---

* If you are interested in developing skills of building rapport, giving feedback and asking great questions, I cover these directly in my other books, *The Coaching Manual* and *Brilliant Coaching*.

1. Connect through effective listening.
2. Build a relationship of engagement and trust.
3. Maintain an effective focus.
4. Help overcome false limits, roadblocks or barriers to progress.
5. Help someone grow.

You might be aware of other tendencies that support effective mentors, such as maintaining a positive outlook, or to regard everyone as having potential. I view these as secondary to the list above, as they are more general abilities (and so less helpful to define a mentor-specific focus), or have less overall impact.

Put aside perfection: let mentors be human

By offering wide-ranging examples of mentor roles (Hagrid from *Harry Potter*, Saul from *Homeland*, Nicole Scherzinger from *The X Factor*, etc.) I aim to show that the mentor role is defined by intention, relationship and circumstance, rather than specific descriptions of skill, knowledge and character. You'll notice that none of the characters mentioned is 'perfect' or above criticism for their personalities or actions. In fact, their flaws and foibles make them more accessible by enabling the people they are mentoring to build an honest relationship with them: their imperfection makes them easier to relate to.

This is good news if you want to mentor others! Where the quality of the relationship a mentor develops is more important than their own perfection, we shift emphasis from 'impressing others' to connecting with them. So please be encouraged by the discussion that follows; use it to build on who you already are and what you already do.

The mentor role is defined by intention, relationship and circumstance

Ability 1: Connect through listening

The ability to create a positive sense of connection to the mentee is fundamental to the relationship and therefore pivotal to the role. By 'connection' I am referring to a personal sense of affinity or even intimacy. I'm aware that responses to the word 'intimacy' can range from neutral to deep discomfort, so it's probably helpful to confirm:

- For you to be a really effective mentor you need to have a level of personal investment in the relationship, e.g. to be engaged in the potential of the mentee to do well and prosper.

- Your relationship needs to have appropriate boundaries, e.g. it needs to be one that blends warmth and commitment with objectivity and discernment.

- Your relationship may or may not feel like a friendship, i.e. the quality of 'friendship' does not define whether or not a relationship is a mentoring one or not. In other words, you may experience a sense of friendship within some relationships and those relationships may or may not have a mentoring element to them.

People who can connect can listen

One of the most direct ways you connect with others is through the quality of your listening during conversation. Please note **we are looking at listening during discussion**, where you might also be talking, asking questions, etc., rather than listening while remaining silent.

In addition to a sense of positive connection, the ability to listen effectively opens up access to many other requirements of mentoring. For example, when you listen effectively you are able to:

- gain a clearer sense of what an individual is saying, e.g. identify the key points or facts being offered

- connect with people personally, e.g. as you increase your focus upon them

- build rapport and relationship quickly, e.g. as people sense they are being listened to, they feel valued by that

- help people communicate more clearly, e.g. as they notice they are being listened to, they can relax and speak naturally

- read the subtle qualities of someone's conversation, e.g. 'What is not being said here?'

- build and display greater empathy as you are able to notice someone's feelings or values, e.g. 'That seems like something that's naturally very important to you'

- adapt conversations to increase relevancy and efficiency, e.g. 'So from what you've said, maybe we need to help you refine where you ultimately want to be, rather than dwelling on your current role.'

Good listening is a combination of attention and intention

We often say that someone is a 'good listener' or a 'bad listener' but this description is too simplistic to be accurate. After all, don't you listen more effectively in some situations than others, such as when it seems important to listen – or not? Does that mean sometimes you are a 'good' listener and sometimes a 'bad' one? It's true that some people typically listen more effectively than others – because they have developed the ability to do that. That's because effective listening is like a muscle you develop over time.

However, what equals effective listening in one situation may not be effective in another. For example, if you are a policeman interviewing a possible criminal, your goals for effective listening might include retaining key information plus a need to spot contradictions. If you are a delegate listening to a conference speaker, your goals may include a need to spot relevance in what's being said to you and your own situation.

What forms your ability to listen is a combination of attention (what we are focused on) and your intention (what your motivation is in that moment).

Effective listening is like a muscle you develop over time

Where is your attention?

Table 4.1 illustrates how the nature of our attention affects both you as the listener during mentoring and also the person who is speaking, e.g. your mentee.

Table 4.1 The nature of attention and its potential impact

Example of attention	Potential impact on the listener	Potential impact on speaker
Scattered, diluted, e.g. 'I'm lost in my own thoughts.'	Reduces ability to receive information. Reduced sense of 'connection' to the other person. Might 'miss' or forget key pieces of information.	May sense a 'lack of listening' and be adversely affected by that, e.g. find it more difficult to relax and speak, over-effort to be heard, etc.
Inconsistent, e.g. 'I'm mostly focused on them but I keep drifting off into my own thoughts.'	Erratic sense of effectiveness, e.g. 'I've got a feeling I'm missing something here' or 'I'm a little agitated'. Perhaps a feeling of 'working hard' in the conversation, e.g. 'Am I getting this?'	Depending on the speaker's awareness, impact may range from minimal, i.e. 'They don't notice', to more significant, 'This person seems distracted'.
Clear and focused, e.g. 'My attention is on this person in this moment.'	The listener feels more connected, both to themselves and to the individual; their mind seems 'lucid' and 'calm'. Thinking processes are paced down, simple and yet seem certain, e.g. 'We're talking about the wrong topic here.'	The speaker is given the opportunity to fully express themselves without distraction, increasing the chances of feeling self-expressed or 'heard'. Will often translate being listened to as a form of being valued by the mentor.

What is your intention?

A person's intention as they are listening may range from positive and constructive, e.g. 'I want to understand you', to much less constructive, such as 'I need to get them to see X', i.e. control the conversation. Please note there are many different possible intentions you might have during a conversation and none of them is 'bad' or 'good' – they just create different outcomes.

Table 4.2 illustrates some intentions that might arise as you listen in a conversation and the impact they might have on you and the person speaking, e.g. your mentee.

Table 4.2 The nature of intention and its potential impact

Example of intention	Potential impact on listener	Potential impact on speaker
'I need to appear knowledgeable on this topic.'	Places focus of attention on the self (rather than the speaker). Puts the listener under pressure, e.g. to think of something 'expert' to say, or to interrupt the speaker.	May sense a 'lack of listening' or 'disconnect' and be adversely affected by that, e.g. find it more difficult to relax and speak, over-effort to be heard, etc.
'I really need to help this person out of this problem' or 'I need to find a solution to their issue.'	Increases pressure to think of solutions/ quick fixes. The listener filters information in/out as they compare and contrast information with their own hypothesis, e.g. 'I wonder if it's this/ that.' The listener may interrupt the speaker's flow, e.g. 'What about emailing them?' or 'Maybe you could just change the appointment?'	Might not notice, or might 'almost' notice, e.g. 'They seem to have an agenda here' or sense a slight misalignment or bias in the quality of listening. May feel less listened to and more 'done to', e.g. 'They keep trying to fix this but they don't understand it because they're not listening properly.'
'I want to understand you.'	Is more focused on the person than the issue and so feels more connected with them. Mind seems 'lucid' and 'calm' as focus is shifted to the other person.	Are given the opportunity to fully express themselves without distraction, increasing the chances of feeling self-expressed or 'heard'. Will often translate being listened to as a form of being valued by the mentor.

Who decides whether intention is constructive or not?

Whether your intention during a conversation is constructive or not is subjective. For example, you might decide a positive intention for your listening is 'I really want to help this person' and yet another mentor may disagree, using the following logic:

- To 'help' someone can feel like rescue – which may disempower them.
- By looking for how you might 'help' them, you might develop a view of your mentee as someone who needs rescuing (by you).
- The on-going relationship may develop the sense of them as a 'victim' and you as a rescuer.

Ultimately, the effectiveness of your listening relates to what is important in the conversation. In the context of mentoring, what is important includes:

- to maintain an effective focus for the conversation, e.g. upon what's relevant and important
- to enable someone to feel listened to, relax a little, trust and be able to discuss topics openly
- to gain an effective understanding of both your mentee and their situations.

Exercise

Notice your intention as you listen

It's sometimes difficult to notice our intention during a conversation as our thoughts can be busy or even scattered. For example, we might feel under pressure or become distracted by thoughts or feelings. So the idea of understanding your intention (or sense of purpose) is less helpful if actually all you're aware of is a feeling of complexity, or 'jumbled thoughts'. The following process can be used to interrupt your mind's 'busy-ness' and help you refocus productively. Try using it during a conversation where you feel a little pressure (but not too much), such as a conversation with someone you find awkward/challenging, or a conversation where you want to create a good impression.

▶

Step One: Notice/acknowledge

During the conversation, bring your awareness to what you are doing in that moment, e.g. 'I'm waiting for them to stop speaking' or 'I'm trying to think of an answer/ what to say', etc. Just notice, that's all, i.e. register what's happening.

Step Two: Check your intention

Identify the intention (or sense of purpose) behind what you were doing, e.g. 'I wanted to have them see my point' or 'I wanted to offer an intelligent perspective'. Make a mental note of this or write it down. Just notice what you appeared to be doing at the time.

Step Three: Review and wrap up

After the conversation has ended; ask yourself the following questions:

Q. How effective was this intention? How much did your intention serve you and the situation, e.g. to be effective in the conversation?

As a final (optional) step, you may decide on a different intention to use in future that may help you be even more effective, e.g. 'first understand what's important to them' or 'stand back from the detail and understand the bigger picture', etc.

Combining attention and intention

For great listening, we need both a constructive intention and focused attention. If we have one without the other, such as a constructive intention but scattered attention, we are still listening less effectively. Figure 4.1 illustrates this idea.

The principle of combining attention with intention is simply to help you become more conscious of what drives you during conversations. By becoming more self-aware, we are more able to change our behaviour and therefore the results we create.

Figure 4.1 Combining attention with intention

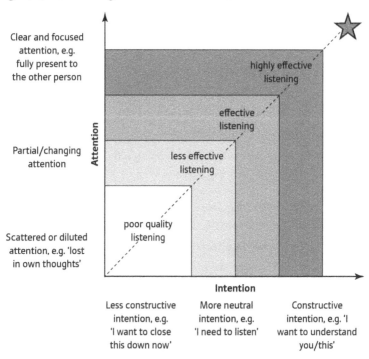

Exercise

Build better listening

To improve the effectiveness of your listening, pick an 'easy' conversation, i.e. an informal discussion with someone you know and trust. Use the following sequence to build better listening.

1 Increase your present moment awareness

First sharpen your attention by staying present to the person/people you are with. By 'staying present' I mean that your attention is on the present moment, you are aware of them, aware of yourself and focused on what's actually happening (rather than on your thoughts about what's happening). As you increase your attention in this way, you will notice your mind naturally 'quietens', i.e. the number of thoughts you are having reduces.

▶

2 Choose a simple intention to encourage effective listening

As your mind naturally becomes stiller/quieter, think of a simple intention and then let it go. Here are some examples you might use:

'Ok, just listen.'

'Relax, breathe, listen.'

'How can I best help this conversation?'

You'll notice that sometimes using a question rather than a statement can be a useful way of engaging the mind in a constructive intention. That's because the mind is drawn towards a question and feels compelled to answer it. Do you find that happens to you?

3 Review what happened

Reflect on what happened. Perhaps write a few notes if that helps, for example:

Q. What did you notice about your listening?

Q. What works for you – and what doesn't?

Q. What's your opportunity with this topic of listening?

Regular practice pays dividends over time

Please know that the process to build better listening can be both tiring and frustrating. Our modern lifestyle encourages scattered attention as we focus on a variety of different activities at once. So be patient with yourself: just keep returning to the simple ideas of shifting your attention, staying present and focusing on the other person. Over time you'll notice your ability to sustain concentration increases as you retrain your wandering mind. As you do this, you'll notice a relaxing of pressure, during conversations specifically. It's also a way to reduce your overall stress levels, as the primary source of stress (your mind) becomes more still.

Ability 2: Build a relationship of engagement and trust

For a mentoring assignment to be successful, as a mentor you need to build a position of positive influence in your relationship with your mentee. This positive influence is best built on a foundation of engagement and trust. Where both engagement and trust are lacking, i.e. the mentee doesn't trust the mentor or is not motivated to learn from them, the consequences of that impact on both the quality of the sessions and the growth and learning of the mentee.

> You need to build a position of positive influence in your relationship with your mentee

Story Teller

A missed opportunity

Michael quite liked his mentor Elaine and respected what she had achieved, but he felt he 'didn't really know her'. She appeared quite reserved, for instance she appeared to 'hold back' certain personal and professional information. Elaine also didn't ask for feedback, which to Michael suggested that she didn't want it.

After some soul searching, Michael decided he should look for roles outside of the company as he couldn't see many career options to progress internally. When Michael was approached by a competitor, he considered telling Elaine but decided it was too much of a risk, as there was long-standing rivalry between the two companies.

When ultimately Michael accepted an offer from the rival firm, it was standard policy that he left his desk the same

> day. As a result, many people, Michael's boss, his colleagues and Elaine, were hugely disappointed to lose someone who clearly had a bright future ahead of them. The opportunity to explore his concerns and options with his mentor didn't happen and Michael left with an incomplete sense of the situation, e.g. 'What if I'd made my feelings more known?'
>
> Elaine never really understood how she had missed Michael's concerns, or why he felt he couldn't be more open.

Here are some simple things you can do to encourage engagement and openness in your mentoring relationships:

- Discuss the topic of confidentiality up front, e.g. confirm that the content of your discussions will be shared with no external party, except by prior agreement.
- Outside of sessions, maintain integrity, e.g. use the principle 'I won't say anything about my mentee that I wouldn't be comfortable to have them hear afterwards'.
- Be willing to share some personal information and data, e.g. about your partner, family, interests, hobbies, etc.
- Understand what drives and motivates your mentee; get to know them, their likes, dislikes, etc. Existing profiling can help, e.g. Myers–Briggs or similar.
- Review the effectiveness of the mentoring discussions regularly, e.g. 'How are these discussions meeting your expectations?', 'What's working/not working, etc.?', 'What else do you need?'

A willingness for disclosure and humility

The need for personal disclosure is another feature that distinguishes mentoring from other types of relationship. A mentor needs to be comfortable sharing the flawed reality of their experiences, knowing that to 'gloss over' failures, setbacks or mistakes is probably unhelpful for the mentee. A good mentor will often choose openness rather than protecting a professional façade, e.g. 'Looking back, getting sacked from my first management position was probably just the wake-up call I needed.'

As with the quality of benevolence or personal commitment, the level of sharing you engage in should be beneficial to the mentee. For example, a mentor might describe how having children has affected her outlook and her career and that might be helpful. However, if the same mentor uses the topic to express anger and vitriol at the organisation for what she feels is unfair treatment of mothers, that's less constructive. A male mentor might tell a mentee how in his youth he prioritised work over his family, costing him his first marriage, as a way of encouraging a greater sense of balance. However, if the same mentor dwells on the experience for longer than is necessary to highlight the point, or allows himself to become upset while talking, then the helpfulness of the story is likely to be lost. The purpose of any mentoring conversation is to benefit the mentee in some way and the link or relevance back to them must be maintained.

When an appropriate balance of disclosure is maintained, it can serve to reassure the mentee and also inspire confidence. For example, when they realise that you have overcome your own challenges and setbacks, they may look at their own fears and concerns more objectively.

> *I am struck by how sharing our weakness and difficulties is more nourishing to others than sharing our qualities and successes.*
>
> Jean Vanier, philosopher

Ability 3: Maintain an effective focus

The need to maintain an effective focus spans both individual mentor conversations and the overall assignment. By effective focus I am referring to a need to:

- help to identify what is important for your mentee to work on, i.e. their priorities
- facilitate conversations with your mentee in a way that helps them to gain the most value from those conversations
- keep sight of the overall assignment themes, e.g. career development, building confidence, etc., within individual mentoring conversations
- notice distractions or 'conversational wandering' that are likely to be counterproductive or unsupportive of your mentee's progress
- encourage a focus on topics that benefit your mentee's ultimate success, including those that might be challenging, e.g. your mentee's tendency to procrastinate, or avoid confrontation
- stay flexible and creative within conversations, to maintain challenge and progress (avoid unhealthy repetition or routine).

Mentoring does not happen in a vacuum, it happens as part of real life. Mentoring assignments often begin well (helped by enjoyable discussion of intentions, goals and a general sense of optimism). They then continue against a backdrop of everyday events, challenges and change. These unexpected elements may then cause the conversations to shift emphasis, or alter in nature. This is not a problem but merely a potential 'pitfall' you need to be comfortable with. Also, as warmth and 'ease' within your relationship build, there is an opportunity for your conversations to wander, drift or simply become 'cosy'. For example, your discussions get distracted by story telling, or as you both try to fix everyday issues. In the diversion, the initial intentions of the relationship can get lost.

Mentoring does not happen in a vacuum, it happens as part of real life

These natural developments require you to keep sight of the overall intentions of the relationship, while staying flexible enough to navigate effectively as circumstances change. For example, a relationship may begin with a desire from your mentee to develop a better ability to handle pressure and a greater tolerance for taking risks. Between sessions, their business partner quits and they are left running a busy tool-hire business on their own, which puts their expansion plans on hold. As a result, your mentee wants to use the 'safe space' of the mentoring conversations to recount stories, express concerns and share feelings. As a mentor, you have a balance to maintain:

- You want to maintain the relationship with the mentee, e.g. promote trust and engagement.
- You need to keep sight of the stated goals of the mentee and encourage awareness of those, e.g. increasing the mentee's tolerance for pressure and ability to take risks.
- You need to be open to adapting the focus of the assignment if that is appropriate.

Using the previous example, your mentee needs to decide whether the split with their business partner is a distraction or something to incorporate. Where your mentee appears to be using the sessions to 'download' a stream of thinking or vent emotion, then an element of that may be useful. For example, if your mentee spends the first part of a conversation updating you as to what's happened since your last session, this can help them clear their thoughts and relax a little. It's also likely that everyday events present 'enablers of learning' to which you can make links in the mentoring conversation. For example:

- 'I can see a real opportunity here for you to reshape the business more towards how you said you want it.'
- 'This situation actually matches your development themes perfectly, doesn't it? I can really get that.'
- 'For me, the development links to your goals of handling pressure and taking risks, which is interesting.'

Alternatively, you might use the situation to help facilitate the mentee's thinking, for example:

- 'How can your partner leaving actually help increase your ability to handle pressure?'
- 'How does this relate to your goal of taking more risks?'
- 'How might this be the perfect event to support your development themes right now?'

In this way, you can also test whether there is, or is not, a link back to your mentee's initial goals. If there is, then great, you can continue. If you find there isn't, then your option is to keep going, in the hope that everything will work out, or make an observation, such as:

- 'Can I just check back to confirm what you want my help with? We talked about handling pressure and taking more risks – is that still something you're interested in?'

Whether or not your mentee preserves their initial topics/themes for the relationship is less important than you retaining sight of what themes they want to work on. So it's okay for your mentee to switch or adapt the topics/themes that they want help with, but as their mentor, you need to stay aware of this, so that you can shift your own focus as appropriate. A little like altering course on a journey, you'll want to know which new set of stars you now need to navigate by.

When does 'I'm helping them to stay focused' equal 'directive' or 'controlling'?

By using phrases such as 'help them' or 'encourage' or 'facilitate their thoughts' we raise the question: as a mentor, how much should you influence the direction and/or content of conversations? For example, your mentee says they want to understand more about leading teams during restructure and change. So you explain your views on this, plus share some stories from the past. However, your mentee appears to focus on the less relevant points of discussion, such as who you used to work for, what they were like as an employer, etc. You may become confused or even frustrated by what you see as a distraction, as the key points you want to make relate to the challenges of the change you implemented and what you learned from that. You want to maintain an effective focus and this doesn't appear to be effective to you. However, you also know that, ultimately, what your mentee learns is up to them and this principle must be balanced with your desire to stay focused.

In the previous example, you need to understand:

- Did what they want to know about (their agenda) just change?
- Is it possible they have good reason for the apparent digression (being interested in your previous employer)?
- Are they simply distracted (perhaps because they tend to have difficulty maintaining focus)?

Once you understand what is behind their apparent digression, e.g. it's a firm they have wondered about as a potential employer, you can return to a principle of 'support and assist them'. However, you also need to be aware of your own motivation at that point in the conversation, i.e. when you shift from an intention to 'support and assist them' to 'I personally need to have them "get" something'. In the previous example, you may want to cut short the conversation about your old employer and return to the topic of managing change, because that's something you personally feel they need to get better at.

It is your intention more than your behaviour that will help you understand if you are being overly controlling in a conversation. To raise your awareness of your intention during conversations, use the exercise 'Notice your intention as you listen' earlier in this chapter.

Have opinions, offer them, then remain unattached to them

To be clear, there's nothing wrong with having a view of what your mentee should be focused on. Perhaps they are using a conveniently interesting coincidence (that you used to work for someone they are interested in) in order to avoid a more challenging topic (managing change). It's also helpful to maintain an objective position with your views, and stay unattached (neutral) as to whether they accept your view or not. One way to do this is to offer your view as an observation, e.g. 'I wonder if we're getting side-tracked here – are you still interested in managing change?' or 'We seem to have gone off the topic here – why is that do you think?'

The more attached we are to our views, the more 'blinkered' and dogmatic we become. This means we are often unaware of a better viewpoint, gained by our open mind. This means that we can be unaware of a better viewpoint or that would have been available to us, had we retained an open mind. Also, where we want people to be able to decide things for themselves (and actually they usually want to do that anyway), our 'strong views' can cause people to reject them automatically, sometimes known as a 'polarity response'. For example, if I say you really shouldn't be interested in other employers right now, don't you immediately think, 'Why not?' However, if I say, 'Maybe talking about a potentially great company to go and work for is simply a way of avoiding tackling the issues that face you right now – what do you think?', does that soften your resistance to the idea a little? Anyone parenting or working with young adults will have direct experience of this, e.g. sometimes it's better to offer an idea than give a direct piece of advice. That way someone who is strong-minded (strong-willed) is less likely to reject it instantly as something that's not theirs. Instead they can consider it for themselves and perhaps during that process of consideration, it becomes 'theirs' after all.

The more attached we are to our views, the more 'blinkered' and dogmatic we become

Ability 4: Help overcome false limits, roadblocks or barriers to progress

If the mentor is a travelling companion for part of the mentee's journey, then some of the function they perform is to help remove roadblocks to the mentee's progress along the way. For example, Dumbledore gives Harry Potter the 'Cloak of Invisibility'. The cloak helps Harry overcome physical barriers to access dangerous places and gain information he needs to defeat Voldemort. In the film *The Karate Kid*, Mr Miyagi teaches Daniel karate skills that help him overcome barriers of ability and low self-esteem.

For the modern-day mentee, examples of the blocks and barriers that you might help them overcome include:

- professional awareness, e.g. how do I read a profit and loss account? Or, what is the difference between creativity and innovation?
- connections, relationships, e.g. having a network of people who can link them to opportunities or assistance
- barriers related to limited thinking or beliefs, e.g. 'I can't build a business on my own because I don't have the right education/experience/background.'

As a mentor, how you help remove barriers to your mentee's progress requires flexibility on your part to stay open to a broad range of approaches. Table 4.3 on the next page uses the above examples to indicate some of the options available to you.

Sometimes your 'assistance' is to prepare the mentee for challenges

As a mentor, your role is often to prepare the mentee for future challenges, perhaps by teaching guiding principles, or helping them build a broader base of skills, contacts or experience. Where this is the case, your involvement must be guided by the intentions and goals for the assignment, in combination with your own view of what's right to do. This sense of 'what's right to do' can be strengthened by the guiding principles in Chapter 3.

Table 4.3 Dealing with barriers to a mentee's progress

Apparent block or barrier	How as mentor you might help remove this	Comment
Professional awareness. How do I read a profit and loss account? Or, what is the difference creativity and innovation?	• Through discussion, e.g. explain ideas, share stories, offer personal insights and perspectives. • Introduce them to information or learning experiences, e.g. book recommendations, people, etc. • Invite them to a session, conference or meeting where they might gain further insight into the topic.	In these examples, your involvement in 'assistance' gradually increases, e.g. moves from you simply talking to you actually doing something.
Connections, relationships, e.g. having a network of people who can link them to opportunities or practical help.	• Facilitate their thoughts, e.g. 'What kind of people do you need to find?' • Give advice, e.g. 'I think you need to join something more formal.' • Introduce them to the mentor's own network, e.g. 'Let me take you along to this event.'	Again the level of your involvement increases with the three methods.
Barriers related to limited thinking or beliefs, e.g. 'I can't build a business because I don't have the right education/ experience/background.'	• Share personal views/stories, 'Yes, I used to think that' or 'I disagree and here's why,' etc. • Help facilitate their thoughts, e.g. 'Let's look at what is actually stopping your progress and what isn't.' • Offer knowledge, e.g. 'Here are the options you have/here's what you can do.'	The range of 'helping' here is broad and begins with 'do very little' (let them figure it out themselves) and moves to 'get more involved'.

Sometimes the mentee cannot foresee their own challenges

Imagine your local university runs a mentoring scheme to support people on a business management course. As a volunteer mentor, you are given a half-day introduction to mentoring and afterwards assigned to a mentee. They are a small business owner about to launch an online website selling pet products with an emphasis on dogs and cats. They currently run a wholesale version of this business, selling their products to pet stores which then sell to the consumer (customer). You currently run a call centre for a busy car-hire business and have lots of experience in dealing with customers and managing during periods of business change.

At your first session, your mentee explains that their pet products have been successful and they now want to grow sales and increase profit by selling to the pet owners direct online. They also want to keep the existing business (selling the same products to pet stores). They believe their existing team of three people can handle the new online, customer-facing part of the business, as they think it's likely to start small and grow slowly. They also believe that the processes involved are 'similar, but different'; they explain they've got good people who should be able to take on the challenge.

During the first session you decide that while your mentee is hugely optimistic about the prospect of dealing with customers, they seem unprepared for the realities of how tough that can be. While you could easily focus on 'revising' each of their incorrect assumptions, you know that will possibly waste time. In your view, their biggest apparent barrier to progress appears to be their lack of knowledge and experience and they simply do not have the time to build that from the ground up. Here's the logic you decide to work from:

- Your role is to help them make progress in their current situation and with their current goals.
- Your role as mentor is to empower them, i.e. equip them to deal with future challenges.

- The most significant risk to their progress appears to be their lack of experience of a business that has individual customers at the heart of it (and you're not sure how that risk might present itself).

- Their success will rest upon their ability to sustain positive communication and engagement with their team (as they are relying on their team to make this work).

- If you are to help them, they need to engage with and trust your view.

From the outset, their initial commitment to mentoring appears positive, e.g. at the first session you've agreed intentions and purpose, principles, boundaries and process, etc. However, you are less sure of how open they are to discussing the potential blocks/barriers that you envisage them encountering. These include:

- They are so enthusiastic about giving great customer service that they set expectations that cannot be maintained, e.g. commercially or practically.

- Their current team is inexperienced in the challenges of dealing with individual orders and related customer issues.

- They need to maintain the service and goodwill of the pet stores business while developing an online retail business.

So you begin sharing your views as a way of raising the business owner's awareness, but also testing their attitude to your perspective. You share some experiences of how dealing with customers can complicate apparently simple matters or impact a team's morale. You also gently challenge some of the beliefs and assumptions around adapting to change, e.g. 'It's basically the same business with a few more phone calls' or 'I just need to leave the team to figure it out for themselves.'

While there are many ways you might work together from this point, the principle of helping prepare them for challenges (as you see them) is important. Otherwise, you risk meeting up for either falsely optimistic conversations, or conversations where you attempt to 'fix' the latest problem they are experiencing.

As a mentor, the view you maintain is one of a journey, where the destination is less important than your mentee's growth through challenge and learning. The journey in this case is towards being a business owner who can stay resilient and effective as they lead and manage the business through change. Their growth will come through tackling the challenges of balancing new customer needs with those of their existing customers and their team. A good mentor knows that they need the challenges in order to grow and learn and their role is to equip the mentee to stay resourceful and resilient. They also know that taking away or 'fixing' problems for the mentee may be convenient in the short term, yet will disempower them in the future.

> The view you maintain is one of a journey, where the destination is less important than your mentee's growth

Using wisdom and insight to help remove barriers and blocks

There is no magic formula to define exactly how you should help in situations, but by staying aware and alert – to yourself, the situation and the options – you are likely to make a better, more effective choice. By 'better' I simply mean one that works out well and aligns with mentor principles, such as offering appropriate assistance. Your 'better' choice comes as you gain an understanding and insight into the situation, often indicated as you feel a sense of 'knowing' or confidence in your own view. This might also be described as an expression of wisdom or blending of experience, knowledge and intellect.

We all have access to wisdom and insight and yet it can occur as sudden or profound, e.g. 'I didn't realise I thought that.' Perhaps someone asks you what you think about something, such as what makes a good marriage, a great childhood, or any topic that provokes you to enquire into your experience and beliefs. You may have sometimes surprised yourself either with what you found you believed or with the depth of insight you surfaced.

These moments when wisdom or insight surface tend to happen more when we are lucid, aware and alert. Another way of explaining 'aware and alert' is to stay conscious or fully present, meaning your mind is focused on what's happening now and you have a sense of being 'grounded' or 'in your body' (rather than lost in a mass of thoughts).

To increase your present moment awareness and create more access to insight or wisdom, try the exercise here.

Exercise

Increase your access to insight

Part One: Get present

Take a steady, slow breath in (through your nose) and feel your lungs expand as you do that. As you breathe out, draw your attention to your body, e.g. move your toes, adjust your posture, increase your awareness of your physical self. This takes only a few seconds by the way; it's simply a sense of 'ah yes, here's my body'.

Let your awareness of your breathing and your body help you increase your awareness of the present moment or a sense of 'what's happening now'. Notice where you are and what's happening.

Part Two: Enquiry to encourage insight

Once you have increased your sense of 'being present' your mind will quieten as your attention is focused on what is happening in the moment. You now have the option of enquiring into a challenge or question in order to gain insight relating to that. Let's take your development as a mentor for the topic and use this question:

- To be a better mentor for others, what simple idea do I need to remember?

---

1 Get present (using the previous steps), return to the question and focus on that.

2 When thoughts and ideas arrive, write those down.

3 When you have three or four thoughts or ideas written down, decide which of those you want to act upon.

As you practise this more frequently, you'll find that writing down ideas is less necessary, as you learn to notice clear ideas that you want to act upon. This enables you to use the method in conversation with others, e.g. during mentoring sessions.

Ability 5: Help someone grow

One of the principal functions of a mentor is to help someone grow. By 'grow' I mean that through the process of being mentored a person can:

- increase their knowledge, wisdom and awareness
- increase their sense of maturity, i.e. that they appear experienced and emotionally well balanced to others
- enlarge their view of the world or broaden their perspectives in a way that they can draw upon, e.g. 'Here's another way of looking at this.'

The ability of a mentor to help people grow is a product of the previous four abilities. Growth is less something the mentor can make happen by targeted effort and more something they develop a positive intention towards. So this ability is simple in theory and less straightforward in application, as the ways we help people to grow are both conscious to us and unconscious. For example, you hope that because you've recommended books or audio programmes, you're encouraging learning, but actually your mentee is developing the most from experiencing your 'upbeat, no-nonsense' approach to things.

One of the principal functions of a mentor is to help someone grow

It's also important to confirm that as a mentor, you are not in charge of factors such as your mentee's readiness to learn, their world view, surrounding events, etc. As mentioned previously, mentoring is a collaboration where the mentee, plus everyday events, also play their part. Some features that cause growth cannot be predicted, such as the sudden loss of an important relationship, or having a family, etc. As a mentor you might usefully remember that you are one part of a team. Your function is to operate from the mentoring principles, plus sustain an intention to improve your ability as a mentor. When you know your actions and judgements flow from those two ideas, then you will add value, even if for you it doesn't seem overtly significant.

To illustrate, using the previous example of a business owner building an online pet product business, Table 4.4 shows how their experience will have a growth impact both with and without mentoring.

People can be a bit like trees

This idea of someone 'growing' through the experience of being mentored might be compared to growth in nature. You can hope that the ground is fertile and that the weather conditions are conducive. You can tend to something, e.g. strip away the weeds that mire its progress or give it nourishment. Ultimately, however, there's a subtle element of which you are not in control. Additional effort, such as staring at something, over-watering something or mentally 'urging it on', is redundant. Some plants thrive in the harshest of conditions while others might fail in the lushest of circumstances. As a mentor, when you have followed what you trust is an effective process, guided by what you believe are good principles, that must be enough.

Table 4.4 Impact of mentoring support

Without mentoring support	With mentoring support
The owner's perspectives/ beliefs are shaped by experience, e.g. facing challenges and overcoming them, or having problems and fixing them.	The owner's perspectives are blended with or drawn from the viewpoints of the mentor, e.g. 'What do you think?' and 'So what do I think?'
Learning is mostly self-generated, e.g. by what happens and doesn't happen, or self-reflection caused by own natural tendencies, such as 'I tend to mull things over a lot'.	Learning is encouraged by the increased emphasis and focus created by the mentoring conversations, e.g. as the owner's new role influences the topics discussed.
Personal wisdom and insight are encouraged through internal processes, such as self-reflection and contemplation. This may arise less consciously, as a 'passing thought' or idea.	Wisdom and insight are encouraged by the process of speaking to someone else, and driven by the intentions born from the conversations, e.g. 'What do they think about this and do I agree with that?'

Chapter summary

We recognise great mentors by the impact they have on other people and also by the common tendencies they have within successful mentoring relationships. These tendencies include the ability to:

1. Connect through effective listening.
2. Build a relationship of engagement and trust.
3. Maintain an effective focus.
4. Help overcome false limits, roadblocks or barriers to progress.
5. Help someone grow.

As a mentor, while it is not necessary that you excel in all of the above to make a positive difference, it is important that you stay aware of them. As you stay aware of them, and intend to get better at them, over time they will help you to develop even greater impact as a mentor.

Chapter

5

Sometimes it's the journey that teaches you a lot about your destination.

Drake, musician and rapper

A process to support your journey

In this chapter:

- Learn a sequence of logical stages that supports your mentoring activity:
  1. Set up: prepare to mentor.
  2. Set out: begin, get started.
  3. Navigation: maintain progress.
  4. Set down: consolidate learning.
  5. Parting ways: complete the relationship.
- Break down your activity into 'bite-sized' pieces to approach mentoring in a practical way.
- Deal with your practical considerations, e.g. 'How do I set up the first meeting?'

It's time to get practical and look at the different activities and stages that naturally occur as you mentor someone. If you have skipped the first few chapters to get to here, this section can help you to get started by walking you step by step through the main stages of mentoring someone. What it won't do is answer any questions you might have relating to the nature of a mentor relationship and what makes you effective as a mentor; you'll find those answers in the previous chapters.

These stages of a mentor's involvement will be especially relevant if you view your mentor relationship as an assignment, i.e. a series of conversations with an intended duration. For example, you may agree an assignment to provide mentoring support for a period of 18 months and meet your mentee, in person, every 6–8 weeks, for 90-minute conversations.

If your approach is less defined, then the following process can still improve the impact of your mentoring. It will help you to decide where you need a little more structure and which activities you may not require.

To approach mentoring in a practical way, it's useful to consider it as a journey, i.e. an experience with a beginning, middle and end. This helps break down your activity into specific sections. If you prefer to think in terms of a process, that's fine and will work just as well.

The journey (or process) will describe the stages (or milestones) illustrated in Figure 5.1. Each of the stages follows as independent sub-chapters. Even if you have already begun your mentoring relationships, I encourage you to review the earlier stages of 'prepare to mentor' and 'get started' to see whether there is any activity you have overlooked and from which you might still benefit.

Mentor's Toolkit

In the Online Toolbox, there are the following documents to help you apply the ideas and principles in this chapter:

✔ Reflection note: Prepare to mentor

✔ What is mentoring? An overview for mentees

✔ Prepare for mentoring: Checklist for mentees

✔ First session: Outline agenda

✔ Following a session: Mentor reflection note

✔ Following a session: Mentee reflection note

✔ Second session: Outline Agenda Option A (relationship emphasis)

▶

Figure 5.1 The Mentor Map

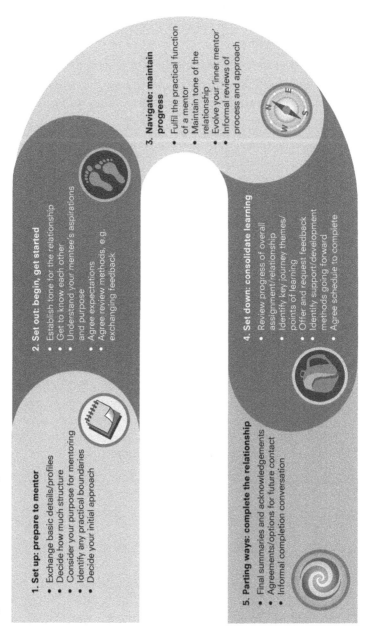

1. **Set up: prepare to mentor**
   - Exchange basic details/profiles
   - Decide how much structure
   - Consider your purpose for mentoring
   - Identify any practical boundaries
   - Decide your initial approach

2. **Set out: begin, get started**
   - Establish tone for the relationship
   - Get to know each other
   - Understand your mentee's aspirations and purpose
   - Agree expectations
   - Agree review methods, e.g. exchanging feedback

3. **Navigate: maintain progress**
   - Fulfil the practical function of a mentor
   - Maintain tone of the relationship
   - Evolve your 'inner mentor'
   - Informal reviews of process and approach

4. **Set down: consolidate learning**
   - Review progress of overall assignment/relationship
   - Identify key journey themes/points of learning
   - Offer and request feedback
   - Identify support/development methods going forward
   - Agree schedule to complete

5. **Parting ways: complete the relationship**
   - Final summaries and acknowledgements
   - Agreements/options for future contact
   - Informal completion conversation

✔ Second session: Outline Agenda Option B (goal and task emphasis)

✔ Review an assignment: Potential agenda topics and questions

✔ Consolidate learning: Potential agenda topics and questions

You'll find these documents as free downloads online at starrconsulting.co.uk

Mentoring as part of an organised scheme

If you mentor as part of a mentoring scheme (perhaps something led by your organisation or run by your local university, etc.), it's likely that a supporting process and principles are already available to you, or even a requirement for you to follow. The amount of structure used in mentoring schemes varies: most schemes appoint coordinators to 'match' mentees to mentors, while some encourage mentees to find and approach their own mentors. In organisations, potential mentees are often people identified as 'talent'/'high potential' or requiring development. Some organised schemes have formal reviews and assessment mechanisms, such as structured interviews or electronic questionnaires, while others are happy to gather anecdotal feedback as an indication of effective relationships.

Potential mentees are often people identified as 'talent'/'high potential' or requiring development

Even if you are part of an organised scheme, it may still be useful to review what follows to see whether there are any additional ideas you might benefit from. It is my intention to add to or enhance the support and guidance you have available to you, rather than replace that in any way.

5.1 Set up: prepare to mentor

Activities at this stage include:

- exchange basic details/profiles with your mentee
- decide how much structure you want to encourage
- consider your purpose for mentoring
- identify any practical boundaries you may have (location of meetings, etc.)
- decide your initial approach.

Whatever your reasons for mentoring, you will be more effective if you are clear on how you will approach that activity. This stage ensures that you are equipped to begin well and continue in the same way. I will assume that you are aware of who you are going to be mentoring and have been already connected/introduced to them. Perhaps they have approached you, or you have been introduced by a third party. If you are part of an organised scheme, you might have been 'matched' with them by the coordinator of that scheme. This section is to help you consider your approach to mentoring, to increase your clarity and confidence, while building a base for success.

Reflection Questions

Practical preparation

Use the following questions to help you plan and prepare to mentor someone:

Q. How much do I need to know about my mentee's situation and circumstances, and what understanding do they need of mine?

Q. What is the broader context for this, e.g. who else needs to be involved, are there stakeholders, etc.?

Q. What are my practical considerations, e.g. time, location, medium of communication?

Exchange basic details with your mentee

Before meeting someone, it's a good idea to have an initial understanding of each other, in both professional and personal terms. For example:

- personal facts: contact details, where they live/are based
- professional background and key facts, what job/role they currently have, etc.
- what brings them to mentoring (what is their purpose or intention behind that).

This is not intended to be detailed information but a broad overview of key facts. As a mentor, you want to begin to orientate towards your mentee and perhaps consider how you might be able to support them. You also want your mentee to begin thinking about what they want from you that can help them learn, grow and make progress. A method for doing this is:

1. Email or send a link to a professional profile, or CV.

2. Have a short telephone call or Skype (15–30 minutes).

3. Confirm way forward by email, e.g. 'I'll see you next Thursday at 3pm.'

Reflection Questions

Personal preparation

Before any new mentoring relationship, it helps to clarify your own view and expectations, to build your self-awareness and focus. Use the following questions to help you to do that. If your relationship has already begun, check out the questions anyway and see whether there are any you want to reflect upon now.

Q. What sense of purpose have I got for mentoring this person? (Why am I doing this?)

Q. What are my potential barriers? (What might stop me being successful?) How will I overcome them?

Q. What boundaries might I want to put around this relationship, e.g. my level of involvement, type of assistance I can offer, etc.?

How much structure is best?

The success of any mentoring relationship is increased by building a framework which supports that up front. The balance you aim to strike is to adopt structure in a way that is helpful and not excessive, i.e. avoid constraints of intense formality, rigour or routine. So it's useful to consider how much structure you think you need early on. By structure, I'm referring to the following:

- An understanding of the relationship in practical terms, for example:
  - ◆ 'Let's meet every 6–8 weeks for around an hour' or 'We won't have regular meetings, just call me every few weeks and we'll discuss what's been happening'.
  - ◆ 'We'll meet over Skype and you (the mentee) will schedule meetings to suit both our time zones.'
  - ◆ 'For the next three months we've got a new part of the business going live, which unfortunately means I may have to cancel sessions at short notice.'
- Boundaries/scope of involvement and duration, for example:
  - ◆ 'Let's work together for a 12-month period' or 'Let's just begin and then let's check what you're getting from this, e.g. after six months' or 'You just want support over the period of this project, (so we'll complete when the project does).'
  - ◆ 'As your mentor, here's what I'm assuming that I'm here to do – how does that fit with your expectations?'
  - ◆ 'I'm expecting my involvement to be by sharing experience, offering advice, information, etc.' or 'I may be able to involve you in what I do a little, e.g. have you shadow me at work, etc.'
- Principles to guide the relationship, for example:
  - ◆ 'My purpose is to support you and your career progress, not improve your business results.'
  - ◆ 'Please keep your notes and please be aware I won't put pressure on you to complete your actions or agreements – that's your business. I'm here to support you and actually what you get out of this is up to you.'

♦ 'Let's check progress occasionally. I want to make sure we pick up on any niggles or if we need to change anything.'

In the preparation stage, only you can decide how much structure is best and once you begin working with a mentee you are likely to adapt the approach. To support your thinking further, Table 5.1 illustrates some unhelpful extremes.

Table 5.1 Building the ideal mentoring structure

Too little structure	Too much structure	Mid-point
No understanding up front of each other's background, current circumstances, 'What brings you to mentoring?', etc.	Lengthy interviewing and screening process to ensure 'perfect fit' for each other. Completion of detailed questionnaires. Rigorous analysis of personality profile information.	Swapping basic professional details, e.g. via CVs or online profiles. Initial chat or telephone call to get to know each other a little and agree a way forward.
Absence of any guiding principles to the overall relationship, e.g. both the mentor and the mentee are improvising their approach to building the relationship.	Long lists of principles and value-type statements that create an air of pressure, e.g. 'confidentiality must be assured in writing' or 'disputes in the relationship must be dealt with by a third party'.	Open discussion up front about what will help the relationship to work and what won't. Explore the topic of confidentiality and find out what assurances the mentee needs. Agree what you will do if either party wants to stop the sessions.
No mention of principles or expectations up front as to how you will work together, just begin conversations and assume everything else will work out.	Overly detailed lists of dos and don'ts which create an expectation of formality and judgement, e.g. 'No meetings to occur outside of working hours.'	Productive discussion around key topics, e.g. approach to the sessions, best way to meet, etc. Mentee takes notes and emails them to mentor after session.

Regardless of whether you consider yourself an 'organised' person or not, considering these questions up front, and deciding what you need or want, will help you feel clearer about how to progress. This clarity will benefit both you and the mentee, helping you to relax and enjoy the process. Much of this early preparation work you can do alone, e.g. by reflecting on questions, jotting down a few notes, etc.

5.2 Set out – begin, get started

Activities at this stage include:

- establish tone for the relationship
- get to know each other, explore each other's experience
- understand your mentee's aspirations and purpose
- agree expectations, e.g. schedule of meetings, scope of discussions
- agree review methods, e.g. exchanging feedback.

Here we will deal with the initial stages as you begin to mentor, e.g. the first sessions, setting expectations, making agreements and generally beginning well.

The importance of establishing tone

Where a mentor relationship is easily confused with other one-to-one collaboration, such as coaching, managing or consultancy, it is important that you act from the distinct principles of mentoring from the outset:

- The relationship is one of equality and yet has a natural bias/emphasis upon the mentor.
- The mentor has something that the mentee needs/wants.
- Responsibility for learning, progress and results ultimately rests with the mentee.

I encourage you to communicate these to your mentee by aligning your behaviours to evidence/express them consistently. Table 5.2 illustrates this idea.

Table 5.2 Establishing tone

Principle	Misaligned behaviour	Aligned behaviour
The relationship is one of equality and yet has a natural bias/emphasis (upon the mentor).	The mentor offers little understanding of their perspectives and views during conversations, preferring to take a passive role in the conversation.	While the mentee spends time discussing their situations, the mentor makes links to their own experience, views and beliefs.
Responsibility for learning, progress and results ultimately rests with the mentee.	The mentor personally arranges meetings and sends notes after the session.	The mentee is asked to: • schedule sessions • take notes • complete any agreed follow-up.
The mentor has something that the mentee needs/wants.	Explicit links to what is valued/wanted are not made. For example, the mentor does not mention they have run their own business or have worked with a distinct community of people.	The mentor is comfortable enquiring as to what is valued/wanted, e.g. 'What do you need my help with?' or 'What aspects of me or my story are most relevant to you?'

A positive first session

The first session or conversation in a mentor relationship sets the tone for both future sessions and the relationship as a whole. In addition, much of the way you influence the mentee will be through what you do, rather than what you say, and an effective first meeting can begin that positive first impression. While the success of the first session does not rest upon you alone, you can help it go well with a little advance thought/preparation.

Much of the way you influence the mentee will be through what you do, rather than what you say

For this next section I'm assuming that you have completed the previous stage, 'prepare to mentor', and by now you have:

- some idea of who you will be mentoring – what their occupation is, what their broad circumstances are, etc.

- an idea of the broader context for this mentoring relationship – who else might be involved, whether this forms part of a leadership or talent development programme, etc.

- your personal considerations for the relationship – how often you can meet, how/where it's possible to meet, any scope or boundaries you might want to put around the conversations, etc.

You may also have spoken to your mentee via email or by telephone, and perhaps sent them the overview of mentoring from the Online Toolbox.

Hints and tips

In conversation with your mentee (1)

- Take the pressure off yourself; remember that it's okay just to be in natural, relaxed conversation around topics, e.g. share your views, experiences and beliefs.

- Be encouraging, demonstrate interest and warmth.

- Don't try to explain everything you know about a particular topic. Too much information or opinion is difficult to take in, and often your mentee will retain or act upon a small percentage of what you discuss. Instead summarise your key thoughts and principles where possible.

- In offering any assistance, balance your involvement with a need to empower your mentee. For example:
  - ◆ Offering to write a CV for someone is 'higher involvement' for you but 'lower empowerment' for them (since you have effectively taken the task from them).
  - ◆ Offering to review a draft CV that they write is involvement from you and yet still empowering for them (as they are supported to improve on their own work).
  - ◆ Encouraging them to write a CV without offering to review it is little/no involvement from you and potentially less empowering for them (since they get no feedback that enables them to improve it).

- Avoid setting ambitious expectations of the help you can offer, or giving assurances you later decide that you can't or don't want to fulfil.

- As you become more involved in offering thoughts, giving feedback, telling stories, etc., please avoid an urge to 'fix' or 'solve' what you see as a problem. (Remember to work with the previously stated principles.)

Agenda for the first session

It helps to have some idea of topics and stages for your first conversation to stay both efficient and effective with your time. Below is a draft agenda for your first session and is estimated over a 90-minute time slot. I'm expecting that you will want to shape or change the agenda according to your needs. For example, if you already know each other, then some of the opening 'introduction' activities will be less relevant to you. Or you might choose to adapt (or just ignore) the duration for each item if they're less relevant to the length of your session. Under each item, I've offered additional pointers to help focus the conversation during that item.

Draft agenda: first session

Ref.	Item	Approx. timing	Guidance
1.0	**Initial introductions: Mentor** • Personal facts (age, family, partner's name, education, interests, etc.) • Professional facts (role, previous occupations, key areas of experience and ability) • Anything else that seems relevant	10 min.	You are likely to have shared some of this information already and so this forms a useful confirmation to build upon.
2.0	**Initial introductions: Mentee** • Personal facts (age, family, partner's name, education, interests, etc.) • Professional facts (role, previous occupations, key areas of experience and ability) • Anything else that seems relevant	10 min.	Try to avoid a tendency to stray into 'what I want from mentoring' (that comes later)
3.0	**Highlight areas of connection/crossover** • Where are the similarities or connections (personal and professional)?	5 min.	These are simply acknowledgements: 'Well we both have more dogs than children' or 'We both have project-type roles', etc.
4.0	**Agree the best way to work together practically** • Duration of support (fixed timeframe or open-ended support). • Methods of contact (face to face, telephone or Skype), email schedule and frequency of contact • How you want to review progress of the mentoring, exchange feedback, etc.	15 min.	Where these are already known or assumed (either from an introductory conversation or if you are part of a company scheme), it can help to confirm/clarify these here.

Ref.	Item	Approx. timing	Guidance
5.0	**Identify the mentee's (known) areas of required assistance/support** • What do you want to get from mentoring? • Which topics are you interested in for developing more awareness or ability? • What personal or professional goals are you aware of?	30 min.	These are likely to adapt and emerge more clearly over time. (Please avoid any pressure for them to be 'definite' at this early stage.)
6.0	**Discuss the mentor's potential to offer support in the previous areas** • Here's where I might be able to help (or here's where the connections seem to be). • Here's how I might be able to help (by sharing experience, knowledge, advice or even assistance). • Here's what is less likely, or less obvious where I might be able to help, because I don't have obvious experience or knowledge, or I'm less comfortable, etc.	10 min.	This is a quick 'here's what seems obvious' rather than a detailed offering.
7.0	**Agreements, way forward** • What next, e.g. when and how shall we meet? • What needs to happen between this conversation and that one? • What else do you want to say or ask?	10 min.	Keep this informal and 'light' in tone (remember, you are not their manager).

If you decide to use any or all of the above agenda, please consider offering the topic headings (and key questions) to your mentee in advance of the session. That enables them to orientate to the conversation ahead of time, and prepare their thoughts and ideas for each section. Obviously, you won't need to give them the notes in the 'guidance' column as they are to support you specifically.

What makes a first session positive?

You'll notice that there was little content in the previous agenda that relates to detailed discussion on specific topics, issues, challenges, etc. Remember your initial intentions are to build a framework for a relationship, rather than to tackle specific personal goals and topics that they are interested in. While the above agenda may occur as a significant investment of time, over time the relationship will benefit from the mutual clarity of information, awareness, etc. that you have created. Where your mentee is keen to talk about specific situations and challenges, this can feel like a 'delaying activity'. One option to counterbalance the sense of not actually talking about their 'content' is to schedule the second session shortly after the first, e.g. a week or so later.

Checklist

Features of an effective first session

✔ You shared an overview of your background – professional journey, a little of your upbringing, family construct, etc. – and you have gained an understanding of theirs.

✔ You offered an opportunity for them to begin to get to know you as a person – your likes, dislikes, sense of humour, etc. – and you have begun to do the same with them.

✔ You discussed principles of how you'd like to work together, including how you will review the progress of the relationship and exchange feedback.

▶

> ✔ You gained an initial understanding of what brings them to mentoring, e.g. their sense of purpose in doing this, their aspirations or goals.
>
> ✔ You built a sense of where and how you might be able to help/support them, e.g. 'It's most obviously in these areas.'
>
> ✔ You left with appropriate conclusions and agreements, e.g. the way forward, what happens next, the next session, etc.
>
> ✔ You feel positive about the opportunity, e.g. of their situation and the links to your own experience, views and ability.

Make personalities less important than the relationship

Please note, it is less essential to leave a first session with a sense of 'I think we really like each other' or 'I thought we were a really good match, we've got exactly the same sense of humour, etc.'. While those factors might be conducive, they are not required for the relationship to have had an effective beginning. Here are three reasons why:

1. What drives any relationship that endures over time is our on-going commitment to it, and that must go beyond the 'cosmetics' of initial impressions or personality.

2. The quality of 'liking' someone can be temporary; as we get to know someone we notice other things about a person, such as their values or habits, so this quality of 'liking' may change over time.

3. If you like someone a lot, or even too much, your effectiveness as a mentor may be compromised, so that you do not want to offer tough feedback messages, or disappoint them by refusing a request, etc.

Reflection Questions

Understand how you might help

Use the following questions to help you reflect on the nature of the assistance that you might offer your mentee. The questions work especially well following your first one/two meetings but can be used at any point in the relationship.

Identify what they need your help with

Q. Thinking about your mentee, what do they most need help with, e.g. handling conflict or making decisions or coping with pressure?

Q. If you thought about this topic more generally, what principle or belief do you think they most need to operate from, e.g. 'Learn to set boundaries and say "no"' or 'Stay focused on what's really important' or 'Don't sweat the small stuff (keep things in perspective)'?

Q. If they adopted this belief/principle, how would that affect their progress or situations?

Q. How have you learned this yourself, or how has that belief been relevant for you?

Identify how you might help them

Q. What are the different ways you might help them with this?

Q. Of the ways in which you might help, which require you to become the least involved in the situation and which require you to be more involved?

Q. What is the most appropriate way you can help from your perspective as a mentor?

If you are not clear how you can provide appropriate assistance, please relax and know that you are making progress by reviewing the situation and options. It sometimes helps to wait a day or so, then review the questions again to see how your thinking has matured or progressed.

Where so much of what defines great mentoring builds from the quality of the relationship, it's a good idea to remind yourself of how your mentee's sense of relatedness to you is encouraged through your attention and intention during conversation. Perhaps take another look at the 'connect through listening' section in Chapter 4.

Your mentee's sense of relatedness to you is encouraged through your attention

A positive second session

Where the initial meeting focused on laying the foundations of working together, subsequent conversations will build naturally on that. For example, some of the potential formality of the first conversation can begin to fade away as you have begun building rapport, plus mutual clarity of expectations and agreements. The second session can form a flexible template for on-going conversations as you establish a typical sequence or routine. For example, perhaps you always begin with an update since the last session or close with 'here's what we've agreed'. I'd encourage you to adopt a little initial structure even if you decide to let it go soon after. That way you feel less like you are 'improvising' in early conversations. Instead, you are deciding your own way of doing something based on what works for you and what doesn't.

Two agenda options

I have placed two optional agendas for your second session in Appendix 1.

Second session: agenda options A and B

Agenda A emphasises continuing to build the relationship, while Agenda B focuses more on making progress on a distinct development topic. If you're keen to just talk about situations, tasks and actions, it's completely okay to jump straight to Agenda B. However, before you do, take a quick look at Agenda A in case there's anything you want to use from that. Let me also gently remind you:

- Much of your ability to influence comes from the trust and openness you build in the relationship.
- The mentee is often influenced by your general attitude and demeanour and that can be conveyed as you talk about anything.
- Much of your ability to provide appropriate assistance is derived from you knowing your mentee, their preferences and what motivates them.

Agenda B places emphasis on encouraging a 'future-focus' and a more immediate sharing of knowledge, ideas and advice. It has more of a 'transactional' tone to the discussion in that it is less about getting to know each other and more about talking through issues and challenges. This conversation may feel a little like a coaching style of conversation as you are working through distinct topics to generate a sense of the way forward. That's not an issue as long as you retain the mentoring principles:

- Mentoring is collaboration between you, your mentee and everyday life (you don't need to 'fix' everything).
- The mentee is responsible for what they learn (and focus on).
- What the mentee ultimately chooses to do is up to them.

A valid option is to use both agendas in sequence, e.g. Agenda A in your second session and then Agenda B in the meeting after that.

Both agendas again assume a 90-minute conversation, but you can adapt the timings to suit your session length. Simply choose what appears more suitable/relevant, or create your own agenda by using elements of both.

Hints and tips

In conversation with your mentee (2)

Ensure the conversation has a healthy balance of you facilitating your mentee's thoughts and you offering your own. Here's what I mean by that:

You facilitate their thoughts:

- Listen (become quiet).
- Ask open questions (those that begin with 'what', 'how', 'why', 'where' or 'who').
- Reflect/summarise, e.g. 'Here's what you just said ...'
- Check/confirm understanding, e.g. 'Is that why you didn't apply for the role before?'
- Point out links, e.g. 'Isn't that the same message your partner was giving you?'

You offer thoughts/contribute:

- Make observations.
- Give feedback and opinion.
- Challenge their views.
- Tell relevant stories from your own experience.
- Offer ideas/advice.

Using agendas: a need to balance effectiveness with informality

Agendas are a great way of helping you stay focused and effective with your time during sessions. However:

- Agendas can result in conversations being overly formal and professional in tone (and so inhibit warmth/openness).
- They can prevent the conversation from developing more naturally, or simply chatting about what comes up.
- Agendas can make the conversations feel like work and so less enjoyable or fun for both of you.

While in the initial stages agendas can be useful, over time you may choose to drop them, or reduce their formality. For example, at the outset of a meeting you might create a 'rough agenda' together and make a brief note of that, such as:

1. Update: quick catch-up since last session
   - 'What's been happening?'
2. Topics for this session
   a. Going for interviews.
   b. Handling difficult character types.
   c. Staying positive, motivated.
3. Summaries/way forward
   - 'What have you got from this?'
   - 'What have you decided to do?'
   - 'When shall we meet next?'

If you do choose to continue using agendas, ask that the mentee creates them, to ensure they retain responsibility for the effectiveness of a conversation.

5.3 Navigation and maintaining progress

Activities at this stage include:

- fulfil the practical function of a mentor
- maintain the tone of the relationship
- evolve your 'inner mentor'
- informal reviews of process and approach, e.g. 'How's this going?'

Once you have completed the first sessions and have a sense of direction, as a mentor you need to sustain progress while handling twists and turns along the way. The initial sessions are fairly straightforward as you're getting to know each other, agreeing principles, etc. After those, it's fairly natural for a relationship to 'wobble' or lose some momentum as the less predictable parts of the mentor relationship emerge. The purpose of this section is to help you feel equipped, with reference points that guide and sustain you as you travel. So let's assume:

- you have completed at least the first one or two sessions with your mentee; you understand their background, current situation and aspirations, plus you've begun to provide assistance in some way

- you have shared some of your own background, views and learning, as a way of building the relationship and also to demonstrate links to your relevant knowledge and experience

- you're familiar with how the meetings generally feel and what types of topics the mentee is interested in discussing (and those they are less interested in or reluctant to talk about), etc.

It's fairly natural for a relationship to 'wobble' or lose some momentum

Fulfilling the function of a mentor

Your practical considerations are now to fulfil the functional elements of the mentor role while building the relationship. By functional elements, I mean that you:

- be available to your mentee as you have agreed, e.g. to meet up, exchange emails, on the telephone, etc.

- continue to provide appropriate levels of assistance, e.g. share observations, insights, ideas or offer practical help (where appropriate)

- maintain a focus on their development areas and/or goals to help support their progress towards those, e.g. by highlighting opportunities, identifying blocks/obstacles, etc.

- encourage occasional reviews of the relationship and process, e.g. 'How's this going?'

- maintain a flexible approach by challenging yourself, e.g. 'Am I fulfilling the role?'

Clearly this part of the process becomes the real substance of both the relationship and the progress made by your mentee. The practical elements of your relationship will vary according to the distinct nature of your situation and that of your mentee. There is no 'right way' – there is only what works for both of you. For example, some people will prefer meeting face to face, while others prefer to have telephone calls. Some mentees will enjoy meeting over video-link/Skype, while others may resist that.

Each mentoring relationship builds differently and what is right in one situation may not work in another. The possibilities for the approach you take and then what happens are boundless. For an illustration of the variety of ways your involvement with a mentee might begin and then develop over time, see Appendix 2: Schedule and nature of a mentor's involvement.

Maintain the tone of the relationship

Following on from the outset, you want to maintain an appropriate balance and tone within the relationship. By that I mean that you sustain the relationship as a mentoring one, i.e. as something that is distinct from any other type of relationship the mentee may have, with their manager, colleagues, friends, etc. We do this by aligning our behaviours in accordance with the key principles:

- Mentoring is a collaboration between you, your mentee and 'everyday life'.
- Ultimately, what your mentee chooses to do, learn or ignore from the mentoring conversations is not the mentor's business.
- Some results of mentoring can be identified or measured, while some results cannot. (This does not mean they are insignificant or less important, it simply means you are less aware of them.)

These principles will help guide your behaviours and responses as you continue to mentor someone. Table 5.3 illustrates this idea.

Table 5.3 Maintaining balance and tone

Principle	Misaligned behaviour	Aligned behaviour
Mentoring is a collaboration between you, your mentee and 'everyday life'.	The mentor encourages conceptual discussions re the mentee's stated development themes, while the mentee seems to want to focus more on what's actually been happening, problems, issues, etc.	The mentor uses everyday challenges to link back to development themes and place principles in context, e.g. 'Being given a larger team is actually perfect if you look at your goal of moving to a more generalist manager role.'
Ultimately, what your mentee chooses to do, learn or ignore from the mentoring conversations is not the mentor's business.	The mentor reminds the mentee regularly of actions and feels 'tetchy' at what they see as lack of commitment to progress. They feel there is something 'wrong'.	The mentor remains interested (and not invested) in what the mentor is doing/not doing outside of the sessions. They offer feedback when appropriate, e.g. if the mentee complains at lack of progress, or at scheduled feedback/review points.
Some results of mentoring can be identified or measured, while some results cannot. (This does not mean they are insignificant or less important, it simply means you are less aware of them.)	The mentor maintains a close check on 'results', e.g. they ask their mentee's manager if he/she has noticed any changes since they began mentoring them. They regard their own effectiveness as a mentor to be related to the success of the mentee, e.g. as they gain promotion, enlarged job role, receive offers, etc.	The mentor maintains a broad view of the mentee's progress, e.g. they notice how their mentee appears more optimistic, or their view on situations appears more objective. When setbacks occur, they encourage the mentee to view them as an opportunity to review, reflect and refocus. They are relaxed about what happens outside of sessions, e.g. they are interested yet accepting.

Let the structure support balance and tone

When used in proportion, the structure outlined in this mentor process can also help sustain an appropriate balance and tone to a relationship, e.g. appropriate use of simple agendas to support meetings, occasional reviews of progress, etc. Where you use a little structure in combination with the behavioural principles, the relationship is likely to develop appropriately in nature. We'll cover things that can prevent or inhibit this from happening more directly in Chapter 6, where we deal with pitfalls within mentoring.

Evolve your 'inner mentor'

Being a mentor to someone is more than the practical elements of the role, such as being on time for meetings, offering great ideas and remembering to send a web link or reference point after the session. Remember, what makes mentoring distinct from coaching or consultancy is the nature and intention of the relationship. For example:

- You are personally invested in supporting the learning and progress of someone else (your mentee).
- You focus your efforts in a way that enables the mentee to develop or gain most directly from the relationship.
- You operate from a sense of benevolence towards the mentee, i.e. that you would like to see them succeed.
- You gain the respect of the mentee in a way that enables them to be influenced by you (and it is not essential that the mentee 'likes' you).
- You support the mentee to remove blocks or barriers to their progress, e.g. of awareness, skill or connections.

The activity of mentoring others will inform and develop your skills as a mentor because you will naturally learn through experience. However, your development can be accelerated by additional activities, for example:

- Engage in your own development and learning – read books, watch TED talks, read relevant articles, attend courses, etc. to broaden your world view.

- Get a mentor yourself so that you learn how it feels to be mentored by someone and also what works and what doesn't. (I recommend your development themes do not include becoming a good mentor, so that your experience is one of purely being a mentee.)

- Notice classic mentor relationships in novels, films and stories and then decide for yourself which qualities you most relate to. (The following exercise will help you use your insights from doing that in a practical way.)

Exercise

Evolve your 'inner mentor'

Think of a mentor character who might be real/known to you, or a classic mentor from film, books or stories. You can use one of the earlier examples, or decide upon your own. The exercise will work better for you if you choose a mentor with whom you 'connect', e.g. you like them, respect them or they inspire you in some way. This is because the exercise works with your intuitive senses rather than creative ideas or fleeting thoughts.

1 Write down the distinct characteristics of your chosen mentor, i.e. what makes them a good mentor? Try to identify 3–5 key attributes, e.g. confident, humble, forthright. Write the attributes in a vertical numbered list (so that you have space to write at the side of each one).

2 Against each attribute, consider how much you currently express that attribute to the person you are mentoring – within the conversations you have had, or simply the overall sense you have of the relationship.

3 Use a ranking of 1–10 to score yourself against each attribute, where 10 equals 'I strongly express this attribute' and 1 equals 'I hardly express this attribute at all'.

4 Next review your scores to decide where you feel you express the attributes clearly and also identify one or two attributes you could improve on.

5 Use the following questions to help you consider an attribute you want to improve on:

a. To express the attribute more clearly, what would you have to do more of/less of?

b. What stops you from doing this currently?

c. If you expressed this attribute more clearly, how might it affect your mentoring relationship?

d. What else might be different, e.g. outside of the relationship?

e. What are you going to do as a result of this exercise?

Reflection accelerates learning

To help you develop your personal expression of the mentor role, it helps if you decide attributes of your mentoring that you want to develop and place attention on them. That might be how you conduct yourself during conversations (listen more, talk more, etc.) or to increase a particular skill such as asking more open questions. By placing attention on something you want to get better at, you increase your self-awareness of your current tendencies, plus gain insight as to how you can learn. Reflection notes are an easy and powerful way to help you learn faster, by hastening the unconscious mind's involvement in the process. By reflection note, I simply mean a 'download' of your thoughts which is prompted by useful questions, e.g.

- How effective was my listening during that conversation – how much did I stay 'present' or focused on them?

- What impact did my listening have, both on me and on them?

- How could I improve my listening next time?

Reflection notes are an easy and powerful way to help you learn faster

The questions provoke your thoughts, and your reflections (the 'download') help your mind to make useful connections and gain insight. For example, the question 'What will I discover about myself by being a mentor?' takes your mind in a direction that is likely to produce a useful thought or idea. Try it now: consider or dwell on the question, then make a few notes of the thoughts/answers that come up:

By being a mentor, what might you discover about yourself?

It's also possible for the mentee to use Reflection Questions to accelerate their learning during the mentoring (these are normally kept private from the mentor). However, I recommend that if you do suggest this to your mentee, you are already using them yourself so you can then engage them through your own experience. For example, after each mentoring conversation, write a short reflection note to confirm your experience from that session.

> *Setting an example is not the main means of influencing another, it is the only means.*

> Albert Einstein

Informal reviews of style and approach

Any mentor relationship benefits from occasional reviews in order to:

- confirm alignment with the mentee's goals or development themes (or highlight a need to adapt them)
- review progress towards the mentee's goals and development themes
- confirm the process, e.g. 'This is our fifth session of twelve, we still need to review your career development plan', etc.
- spot any areas of potential practical improvement, e.g. duration, frequency or location of meetings

- highlight any opportunities to improve approach, e.g. 'Let's stop/start using agendas' or 'Let's focus more on methods and tools', etc.
- give and receive feedback on behaviour and style
- help you to learn and develop as a mentor.

Again, it's your preference as to how and how often you perform these reviews and again your challenge is to achieve balance. Performing reviews too formally or frequently is likely to inhibit both the growth of the relationship and the effectiveness of the conversations. However, if you avoid the topics of 'How well is this going?' or 'What could we improve?', you might miss lurking issues or opportunities to increase your positive impact as a mentor.

Table 5.4 on the next page gives you options to consider.

5.4 Set down – consolidate learning

Activities at this stage include:

- review progress of overall assignment/relationship
- identify key journey themes/points of learning
- offer and request feedback
- identify support/development methods going forward
- agree schedule to complete.

This next stage, of 'setting down', begins the process of drawing your mentoring activity to a close, or of completing the relationship as if, in journey terms, we are approaching the final bend in the road before the home straight. Potential activities to support this stage include the following:

- Complete a review of progress: where is the mentee now in relation to their aspirations, goals and development themes?
- Check the main themes or learning from the journey: what would they say they have got from this, e.g. key lessons, things they'll remember?
- Exchange feedback: for instance, what's worked and what could we have done differently?

Table 5.4 Reviewing the mentor–mentee relationship

Review method and topic	Frequency	Observation
1. Quick check: effective process At the beginning of each conversation, check the process, e.g. 'So this is our fourth session' or 'We said we'd revisit your career plan, didn't we?'	Use at the opening of most meetings.	This helps you stay focused and effective but can also indicate you 'managing' the session – which you may or may not be comfortable with.
2. Quick check: effective conversations At the end of a conversation, ask: 'Has this been useful?' and check for confirmation or potential dissatisfaction.	Use at the close of every meeting.	This gives broad indication but relies on the mentee to feel comfortable flagging a potential issue or sense of incompleteness.
3. Unscheduled feedback: for mentee Offer bite-sized observations, encouragement and also development messages on a regular basis, such as: • 'I think you're staying really constructive around what is actually quite a tough situation and that's impressive.' • 'You seem more annoyed about this than last time we spoke.' • 'You appear to be letting this situation take you into a negative frame of mind – I think that's not helping.'	Regularly, randomly, e.g. during most conversations.	This type of feedback creates encouragement and challenge as a function of the mentor. When done in balance it can be constructive to encourage development and growth. When offered in a less balanced way, it is not so helpful, e.g. all encouragement with no challenge, or vice versa.

4. Scheduled review: approach Agree a future 'checkpoint', such as, 'After six months we'll review how we're getting on' or 'At session five let's check how everything is going'. In advance of that session, agree how you'll discuss it, e.g. 'Let's agree what's working well, less well and what we can improve.'	As agreed	Can work well as a scheduled milestone because it: • encourages a productive focus, e.g. your mentee uses it as a date they want to achieve something by • enables both parties to 'park' potential concerns ('I'll raise that at the review') • gives both parties time to prepare in advance ideas, feedback messages, etc.
5. Scheduled feedback: for mentor • Ask the mentee to prepare feedback, messages, for example: • What do I do that works and you'd like me to keep doing, or do more of? • What do I do that works less which you'd like me to do less of? • What other requests do you have of me?	As agreed during an active relationship or once the relationship is complete.	Can work well where the mentee is comfortable to give development messages to the mentor. If the mentee is less comfortable/confident then perhaps ask a third party (such as a scheme coordinator) to gather feedback on your behalf. Other options are asking for feedback via email or by electronic survey (such as Survey Monkey).
5.1 Scheduled feedback: for mentee • Agree a future 'checkpoint' where the mentor offers more structured feedback, such as: • Here's where and how I think you are making great progress. • Here's how I think you might make more progress. • Here are some additional thoughts or observations I have that may help.	As agreed.	Check whether the mentee wants this type of feedback; remember, you are not their manager and their 'performance' is not something you are responsible for. Offer any development messages or observations and advice with warmth and encouragement, e.g. 'I think if you nail this it might make a huge difference to you.'

- Identify on-going support options: how might the mentee continue to progress, e.g. other learning tools or sources of support?

- Agree a schedule to complete: what needs to happen now, e.g. 'We'll have two phone calls and a final session before the year end'?

Each of the above is an opportunity to create clarity, awareness and agreement. The ways in which you do this range from formal to relaxed. For example, a very relaxed review may be to ask your mentee, 'So how was it?' during a conversation and then chat with them to explore their views. A more formal review would be to give them a questionnaire or ask someone else to interview them on your behalf.

To see how the above topics can be completed during one mentoring conversation or session, see Appendix 4: Consolidate learning: potential agenda topics and questions.

How do you know you're ready to 'set down'?

One benefit of agreeing principles at the start of a mentoring relationship (what you'll work on, how you'll work together, etc.) is that this stage becomes easier to approach. For example, you might have a set number of sessions agreed, or set a milestone date such as a job move or a goal to achieve. If none of these cues is present, then they must come from either you or your mentee. Here are some events that can signal this stage naturally:

- You or your mentee's situation changes, e.g. they quit college and go back to work, or your work location changes.

- Your conversations and interactions feel as though they are of diminishing value to the mentee, e.g. the topics you discuss seem to lack importance or substance.

- Your mentee has achieved a major step forward, such as getting their business started, becoming comfortable at public speaking, etc., and it might be empowering for them to now progress on their own.

Here are some ways that you can encourage this stage to occur:

- Introduce the concept of the relationship as a journey or process (with a beginning, middle and end) and use that idea to understand and agree when seems appropriate to reduce involvement/or complete.

- Make a request to schedule completion, beginning with a 'winding down' if that's appropriate, e.g. 'Let's meet less frequently, with the aim of completing by June/July.'

- Prompt a review of the process, e.g. summarise what's happened, identify progress and understand the point at which it makes sense to reduce involvement/complete.

When is the final bend actually a helpful twist in the road?

Ironically, what appears to be the closing stage of the relationship can become a fresh beginning. As you consider ending the mentoring sessions, you review the overall process and perhaps confront what has not worked or has not been achieved in an objective manner. As issues or missed opportunities surface, you may potentially have the chance to fix these. Imagine that you have reviewed the assignment with your mentee and the following becomes clear:

- The mentee has gained much more value from the sessions than you/they fully appreciated.

- The mentee has gained less value than they had hoped they would and is happy to complete (which may indicate potential learning for you).

- The mentee's development themes and goals have changed/moved on from those agreed in the early stages.

- Some progress has been made on topics, such as making clearer decisions or planning tasks properly to avoid pressure. However, other topics, such as facing their fear of failure, or procrastination regarding their career, remain untouched. In discussion, the mentee realises that actually these are the major barriers to their progress and they are simply avoiding them.

- Faced with the prospect of completing, the mentee decides that they have missed an opportunity and they regret that.

To continue or not to continue ...

If you and your mentee discuss a path to complete the relationship and it becomes clear there is an opportunity for you to continue it instead, then you both have the choice of doing that. Even when you operate within the framework of an organised scheme, it is unlikely that any scheme coordinator would ask that a relationship end simply because a limit of sessions or duration of time has been reached. This is normally something that you and the mentee can agree together, hopefully after identifying the reasons to continue.

To help you consider reasons to continue or complete, Tables 5.5 and 5.6 illustrate the logic you might use. Table 5.5 looks specifically at potential reasons to continue.

Table 5.5 Potential reasons to continue the mentor–mentee relationship

Potential reasons to continue	Observation
The review process highlights opportunities for more topics or themes to work on, and you both feel engaged in the option of continuing.	If there is a lack of engagement/commitment from either party, this is a less obvious indication to proceed.
The review highlights a lack of engagement on the part of the mentee as being the cause for lack of progress. The mentee shows real regret, e.g. they feel they have missed an opportunity and that resisting help is a common tendency for them. They hint that they would like to continue.	The potential success of continuing the relationship might be improved by introducing a little structure, e.g. 'Let's continue for an agreed period and look at the areas of missed opportunity and also perhaps the resistance you describe.'

During the review your mentee gave you feedback that they felt you talked only about successes and this meant they didn't always feel comfortable about sharing things that hadn't gone well. They also explained that some of your advice and tone was a little 'black and white', e.g. 'Get a goal, get a plan – and stick to that.' This meant that when they didn't quite relate to the view, they were unsure as to how to proceed, e.g. 'What happens if my plan or goal isn't perfect?' You accept the feedback and would like to make amends, e.g. demonstrate more openness and empathy. Your mentee says they would enjoy continuing, retaining their original topics/goals as the themes.	There is a potential risk here that the assignment becomes overly biased towards you, the mentor, e.g. your style and responses. For example, you may be over-cautious giving your views, or simply 'not yourself' in conversation. Our guiding principles can help us to navigate. For example: ✔ the responsibility for learning and progress rests with the mentee ✔ the relationship is one of equality, with bias towards the mentor ✔ the mentor must balance 'bias' with humility, e.g. remember that they are a mentor to support the growth and progress of someone else.

Table 5.6 considers potential reasons to complete the relationship/assignment.

Table 5.6 Potential reasons to complete the mentor–mentee relationship

Indications to complete	Observation
While the review has highlighted opportunities for topics that could still be worked on, one/both of you remain uncommitted to doing that.	Where the mentee is uncommitted, the relationship is less likely to succeed. However, if it is the mentor who lacks this sense of commitment, you have the choice to change that. For example: ✔ identify what's causing your lack of commitment ✔ decide whether that's something you can and want to change ✔ decide your way forward.

Indications to complete	Observation
An informal review highlights a lack of benefit/progress for the mentee and yet they explain they love the sessions and would like to continue if possible. You feel that while they enjoy the time spent in conversation, they aren't actually engaged in learning. For example, they often talk about making changes and commit to actions that they don't keep. When you offer this feedback, they disagree with your examples and assure you of their commitment to the process. As you begin the next session, you gain the impression that nothing has changed, e.g. they begin with reasons why they didn't follow up from last session.	The potential trap here is one of continuing due to unsound logic, for example: ✔ you are flattered by the mentee's compliments and so you want to please them by continuing ✔ you assume their lack of action is a result of your lack of skills and that you need to simply try different things and the situation will improve ✔ you take responsibility for their progress, e.g. assume that you need to 'turn the situation around' (and that's not your job).
The mentee explains how much value they have got from the sessions. As a result of the conversations, their objectives or aspirations have changed. For example, they are now less ambitious in their career and yet more ambitious about spending time with their family. The principle of you 'having something that they need' is unclear (as you both can't see what assistance you might provide).	Consider 'pressing pause' on the relationship for a while, i.e. agree to discontinue and then review the decision at a later date. Reasons for this include: ✔ the mentee has benefited from the relationship, e.g. they reshaped their priorities between work and family ✔ the shift in priorities may be a temporary one (they might change their mind) ✔ while the collaboration is not able to work right now, it may work well again in the future, e.g. as circumstances change.

5.5 Parting ways: complete the relationship

Activities at this stage include:

- final summaries and acknowledgements
- agreements/options for future contact
- informal completion conversation.

Remember that while a mentor relationship has the option of being unbound by a duration or life span, it is likely to be more 'active' or relevant for a distinct period of time. Consider Ebenezer Scrooge in *A Christmas Carol*. In Dickens' classic tale, Ebenezer Scrooge is taken on a journey into his past, present and future and encouraged to reflect on his behaviours and, importantly, his beliefs. During his 'visitations' and in the company of the three ghosts of Christmas, he faces fears, overcomes personal limits and makes difficult decisions to emerge as a transformed character. Along the way, a mentor (or three) is on hand to guide, illuminate and 'help'.

It's a convenient example to illustrate the point, yet if you reflect upon your own mentors in life, perhaps you can find some resonance with this idea. By this I mean that we are in active relationships with our mentors over a distinct period of time and yet their influence continues beyond that. After that time period, the mentee continues along their path, with the experience and learning from the relationship to draw upon (and the free will to discard that). Where one of your intentions as a mentor is to empower someone else, this stage of completing the relationship becomes a natural requirement of the role.

We are in active relationships with our mentors over a distinct period of time and yet their influence continues beyond that

There must be an end before a beginning.

Anon

This section will give you guidance on how to end the active part of your mentor relationship, as you stop meeting, having conversations, or regular contact to discuss your mentee's progress. Of course, this does not mean you can never see them again, exchange news or give them any type of support, just that you are acknowledging the end of a phase where you agreed to provide active support and assistance.

So let's assume that you have completed the previous stage of setting down and consolidating learning and now have:

- a good idea of what progress your mentee has made in the period of time that you've been actively mentoring them
- some links to how you have provided benefit, what you did that made a difference to their progress, etc.
- a sense that it's okay to complete, e.g. that they are comfortable to continue forward, understand their support options, etc.

The natural sequence is then to complete the relationship, by which I mean:

- leave both parties aware that the active phase of mentoring has ended
- have both parties aware and accepting of why it's appropriate to do that now
- create an appropriate sense of something ending, and therefore something else beginning.

As usual, you have options as to how you'd like to do this, from informal to formal. These include:

- meet socially, have an informal conversation just to catch up, socialise a little and acknowledge the relationship is complete
- meet a little more formally, e.g. book a meeting room, catch up since the previous session, discuss the future beyond the mentoring activity and exchange farewells

- send an informal card, letter, email or similar just to summarise key points, acknowledge the relationship completing, give good wishes for the future, etc.

A 'wind-down' can also work

With some mentees it may work better for you to reduce the activity of the relationship over time, rather than indicate a definite end point up front. This works well where the mentee has grown to really rely on the relationship and feels uncomfortable at the idea of it ending. In practical terms this means:

- gradually reduce the amount of contact and communication you have with the mentee
- increase the time period between conversations/sessions
- steadily reduce the assistance that you offer or provide in situations, either by gently refusing requests or encouraging them to act for themselves in situations.

Winding down or completing can create a little discomfort for either party as the relationship begins to feel a little less close and perhaps more distant. That's why it's important to remember our intention to empower the mentee, by having them feel equipped and resourceful to act alone in situations. We'll look at the potential issue of dependency (both from the mentee and the mentor) more directly in the next chapter.

No ceremony, no pressure, just relaxed conversation

To offer a formal agenda for a conversation at this stage feels inappropriate. After all, if your relationship has evolved from the principles of the mentor archetype, then by now you will know each other well enough to meet without the need for formality. The outcomes from this stage are very simple and will work best when they happen with a natural sense of lightness. In the previous stage, 'setting down and consolidating learning', you have fulfilled the 'task' or 'structure' parts of the relationship. So please relax in the knowledge that you have nothing to get done and can only get this right!

By now you will know each other well enough to meet without the need for formality

Does any relationship ever truly end?

Since being in a relationship with someone does not require you to be in the same physical space with them, the notion of being in a relationship with someone is born from your perception. Logically, a relationship ends only when you imagine it to, i.e. by not thinking of someone or having any feelings associated with them. Perhaps a relationship truly ends only when in your mind someone is no longer part of your world. Imagine your favourite teacher or friend at school, or someone you really liked but lost contact with. As you imagine them, are you not still related in some way? This is why we talk of 'completing' the relationship rather than ending it. By completing it, we are saying, 'this is done and needs nothing more'. Yes, the 'active' part of it is done and you may view it also as 'ended', which is perfectly acceptable, but the choice is always yours.

So while you may have practically ended the active part of the relationship, whether or not it has truly 'ended' is ultimately up to you.

Chapter summary

Relating the active phases of a mentor relationship to a journey is useful in order to create a sense of sequence/structure to the stages the relationship will naturally go through. The stages of an active mentor relationship are:

1. Set up: prepare to mentor.
2. Set out: begin, get started.
3. Navigation: maintain progress.
4. Set down: consolidate learning.
5. Parting ways: complete the relationship.

How much formality and structure you use to underpin the above stages is a question of personal choice. Increasing use of structure, such as initial agreements, agreeing approach, development themes, etc., can help create clarity and so surety of progress. However, too much structure, such as a need for overly detailed agendas and work plans, can inhibit the natural growth of the relationship. What's important is that you remain flexible to the individual nature of your mentee and the situation in which you are mentoring.

Chapter

It's not what you look at that matters,
it's what you see.

Henry David Thoreau

Pitfalls for the less experienced traveller

In this chapter:

- Learn the potential pitfalls that can reduce your overall effectiveness as a mentor, namely:
  - placing yourself under too much pressure
  - having a personal agenda (strategising)
  - allowing the idea of being a 'mentor' to suggest superiority or prestige
  - low levels of engagement
  - avoiding dependency/mutual dependency.
- Consider your own situations in relation to these pitfalls, e.g. 'How is that relevant for me?'
- Create reference points for yourself, e.g. 'What to do when ...'

Let's look at some natural barriers or blocks on your own journey towards becoming an effective mentor for others – I'm calling them 'pitfalls'. By pitfalls I mean things that you might do, or not do, or habits you might fall into, which will reduce your positive impact as a mentor. While there is a range of potential pitfalls, I've chosen the following as useful for you to consider:

Pitfall One: Placing yourself under too much pressure.

Pitfall Two: Having an agenda (strategising).

Pitfall Three: Allowing the idea of being a mentor to suggest superiority or prestige.

Pitfall Four: Low levels of engagement.

Pitfall Five: Avoiding dependency/mutual dependency.

To make your reading easier, I've broken these into subchapters.

6.1 Pitfall One: Placing yourself under too much pressure

An effective mentor is able to experience an appropriate amount of pressure and still react constructively in situations. An example of 'appropriate pressure' might be that you regard your role as important and one that you want to do well at. Or perhaps you are unsure that you have all the attributes you need to be a good mentor and yet you are engaged in the challenge of finding out. This positive type of pressure motivates you to function well in interactions with your mentee. Positive pressure also helps us to enjoy or relish the activity of mentoring someone, perhaps giving us a heightened awareness or 'buzz' from doing it.

Too much pressure reduces your resourcefulness

When we are new to mentoring especially, it's natural that we want to do well and perhaps we place ourselves under pressure to help us do that. While some levels of pressure are healthy and enlivening, heightened or extreme pressure is much less so. Putting yourself under extreme pressure, such as 'I've got a lot to prove here' or 'I really can't afford to mess this up', is unhelpful. Heightened or extreme pressure can have the following effects:

- It reduces our brain's ability to handle and process information, organise thoughts or make decisions. (Under extreme pressure we simply can't think.)
- It results in less natural (and ineffective) behaviours, such as talking too fast/too much, over-explaining, inappropriate use of humour, etc.
- It creates uncomfortable feelings of tension, fatigue, frustration or even anger.

As a mentor, too much pressure can reduce our effectiveness, as we are less able to stay natural and employ our usual strengths and abilities.

High expectations create heightened pressure

Heightened or unhealthy pressure is often caused by a perceived gap in what we expect or want and how we imagine things actually are. For example, if you expect your home to be clean and tidy and the rest of your family leave it in a dirty mess, you may become stressed about that. However, if someone else sees exactly the same clutter and chaos, it may remind them of fun and family and make them feel at home. This person may be relaxed by general untidiness and perhaps stressed by clean, sanitised environments.

Traditional descriptions of a mentor often include helpful phrases such as 'a wise guide' or 'a voice of experience'. However, these phrases stop being helpful when we extend them to mean that (in some way) a mentor has higher standards than we are able to maintain. Consequently, when we begin interacting with our mentee, we can feel a heightened sense of 'pressure to perform'.

> When we begin interacting with our mentee, we can feel a heightened sense of 'pressure to perform'

Alternatively, you may begin mentoring feeling positive, e.g. 'This is an interesting challenge', and then as you begin to mentor someone you may shift your perspective. Perhaps conversations aren't quite as expected, e.g. the questions your mentee poses seem awkward. Or what you thought you would be helping them with doesn't appear to be what they actually need.

It is useful to identify how our sense of pressure is being caused, in order to create a counterbalance to that. Table 6.1 illustrates potential causes of heightened pressure and options to lessen it.

Table 6.1 Potential causes of heightened pressure

Cause	Option/solution	Observation
A belief that you need to be impressive, e.g. inspirational or charismatic in the eyes of your mentee.	Challenge your own perception, for example: ✔ Ask the mentee what they want from a mentor, or ask other mentors to describe the qualities they feel are important. ✔ Use the mentor process (Chapter 5) to help you build a structure and approach that you can trust will support your effectiveness. ✔ Consider sharing your concerns with your mentee (or someone else you can trust).	This situation is often lessened by time, as the process of mentoring demonstrates what you do that is valuable (and what is not).
A belief that you have nothing to offer a mentee, e.g. 'Why me?', 'What have I got to offer anyone?'	Again, challenge your own thinking, for example: 1. Write a draft profile/CV, or simply list your areas of experience, skills and strengths. 2. Get someone you know and trust to review your list or CV and create clear emphasis on the positive qualities, e.g. 'Where are you being modest?' 3. Find out your mentee's situation, challenges and goals, then create links to your own situations or experience (using your list or CV).	This is often an issue of either reduced awareness or unhelpful thoughts (or both). Once you have created better, more objective awareness, work to build on and support that. For example, after a session with your mentee: ✔ write down all the things that went well ✔ write down the things that you did in the session that were positive, or worked ✔ use the reflection note (in the Online Toolkit) to accelerate your learning and build confidence.

Feeling pressure from external expectations, e.g. perhaps you are expected to improve the behaviour of your mentee or 'fix' them in some way.	Ensure that you have agreed reasonable expectations with people, e.g. what results you hope for, and also explain that mentoring cannot guarantee them. Maintain openness (and so trust) with the mentee, e.g. ensure they are appropriately aware of any development messages. Handle that sensitively and try to make sure that messages are positioned constructively, as opportunities, etc.	Maintain a sense of your integrity in the situation, and also your feelings of empowerment. It's important that you avoid feeling 'underhand' or put in an impossible situation. Encourage external parties to take responsibility for their messages, i.e. that they 'own' those.
Being under more general, widespread stress and pressure (outside of mentoring conversations).	Identify and tackle the general causes of your stress, e.g. your beliefs, behaviour, tendencies, or how you are viewing a situation. ✓ Identify and acknowledge what is still within your control. ✓ Spot what is not within your control that is causing your pressure/stress, e.g. what do you need? ✓ Identify options to get what you need (in order to regain a sense of balance).	Extreme stress is often indicated by a sense of loss of control or inability to cope. So it's important to take action to confirm that you are empowered and can still influence your situation. That action might include explaining the situation to someone who can advise or help, making a request of someone, or asserting yourself more in a situation.

As a mentor, you want to stay resourceful and confident and be able to trust that whatever arises during your mentoring conversations is something you are equipped to handle. Learning to understand then manage your levels of stress/pressure is an important enabler of doing that.

When there's a lot to think about, what do you think about?

During initial sessions especially, there's potential for you to place yourself under pressure, e.g. to meet expectations (either of yourself or from others). When we feel under pressure, it is natural for our minds to become overactive in an unhelpful way. Here are some tendencies of a mind under pressure during a session:

- You become so occupied with thinking that you create a sense of disconnect from your mentee (you become less 'present' to them).
- You over-analyse ideas, which results in your speech being more complicated, making it less easy for the mentee to clearly understand what you are trying to say.
- You may think too quickly, which results in unhelpful behaviours that you are less conscious of, such as rapid-fire speech, poor listening, a tendency to get frustrated, interrupt, etc.

If you recognise any of the above tendencies as your own, your opportunity is to train your attention to become simpler and more focused: a little like adjusting the wide beam of a torch to be narrower, more concentrated and bright. In order to do this, you might do any, or all, of the following.

In advance of the session: 'download' and refine your thoughts

A day or so ahead of the session, make a few handwritten notes to review your thoughts and decide what's most relevant. (The Reflection Note: 'Preparing to mentor' in the Online Toolbox will help you do that.)

During the session: use a framework/agenda to relax

Prepare an outline agenda or tick list of key topics, which will help to assure you get those covered. Once you have them written down, you will:

a. Relax because you don't have to remember the topics.
b. Be able to prioritise/ignore topics from the agenda (as you engage with what's actually happening in the conversation).
c. Gain confidence as you feel more in control of your situation.

Following the session: 'download' and reflect

Within a day or so of the session, write down immediate thoughts and ideas and then review these to highlight anything that seems significant. Again, write handwritten notes to 'download' your thinking, i.e. allow yourself to ponder on the conversation for a while and then jot down your thoughts. To help you, there's a Reflection Note template in the Online Toolbox.

Develop a positive perspective

Developing a positive perspective is important as it will help you to maintain a constructive outlook to cope with the challenges and unexpected developments that arise during mentoring. By positive perspective, I mean a way of viewing your situations that enables you to stay resourceful and not constrained by worry. Use the supporting principles to help you develop a positive view of your involvement and also put aside notions of perfection. For example:

- Much of what creates success in mentoring is the engagement and connection from the mentee and this can be reduced by any 'over-efforting' on your part, e.g. as you appear less your natural self.

- Success does not rest solely on your input; success rests on collaboration between the mentee, you as mentor and on-going situations and events (life).

- While you can be committed to the mentee creating successful outcomes, you must also remain detached from them (as ultimately they are outside of your control).

- Maintain a simple intention to serve the needs of the individual and decide to trust in the overall process of which you are a part.
- Developing mentoring skills is a journey for you as well, and that means you will have your own trials/challenges along the way – overcoming those challenges is ultimately enriching and fulfilling.

6.2 Pitfall Two: Having an agenda (strategising)

This pitfall occurs when a mentor distorts the intention of 'providing appropriate assistance' by adding 'I know what they really need help with' or 'I want to get them to do "x" or achieve "y"' or even 'I'll be really disappointed if they don't do this'. During conversations, these distorted intentions can encourage you to:

- over-emphasise certain topics that you think are important, e.g. the mentee's need to be more assertive, or have a conversation with a difficult individual
- offer a lot of advice or information on a topic (or repeat advice if you feel it hasn't been acted upon)
- listen with an intention to 'fix' or 'improve' (either the mentee's situation or the mentee themselves)
- narrow the conversation to topics you believe are important, rather than allowing a sense of what's important to arise more naturally
- display impatience, verbally or non-verbally, e.g. interrupt, frown, fidget, etc.

Negative behaviours are defined by the result they create

Not all of the above behaviours are by nature ineffective. For example, emphasising a key topic may be helpful for a mentee who recognises their tendency to avoid challenging subjects. Or interrupting may be justified where a mentee is unaware that they are repeating themselves or have strayed from a key topic. However, when the above become regular or consistent patterns of behaviour for a mentor, the impact on the mentee can be as follows:

- They sense the 'narrowed' conversation or emphasised topics and are increasingly uncomfortable with that, perhaps feeling nagged or managed by the mentor.

- The dynamic of the relationship shifts towards coaching or managing and so the potential of the mentor archetype is reduced (see also 'When does mentoring become coaching or managing?' in Chapter 1).

- The mentee's engagement levels reduce as they perceive a gap in what they wanted from mentoring and what appears to be happening.

- Where they respect the mentor, and sense their frustration with them, this may lower their self-esteem or confidence, e.g. 'They think I'm a hopeless case so I must be.'

- The mentee may begin to anticipate sessions with unease, e.g. 'I really don't enjoy these conversations, in fact I'm starting to dread them.'

A mentor's agenda can often develop as they begin to form subjective views or judgement

How does the mentor's agenda or strategy evolve?

It is natural for a mentor to want their mentee to gain positive benefit from their involvement and make progress. However, a mentor's intention can develop into wanting something specific for them, based on their own view of 'what they really need' (such as increased confidence, better self-awareness, etc.). This additional something they 'really need' may or may not be appropriate or helpful. For example, the idea that the mentee requires more self-confidence may be accurate (because they would benefit from that). Yet for the mentor to focus actively upon that issue, perhaps by referring to it, or giving ideas or advice relating to it, is less helpful. By increasing focus upon their confidence, the mentee may feel vulnerable/exposed and their fragile confidence is confirmed (or even made worse).

A mentor's agenda can often develop as they begin to form subjective views or judgement on the mentee's situation. These subjective views will be based on the mentor's own world views and bias. For example, if they regard education as a basic requirement for professional credibility and their mentee has relatively few qualifications, the mentor is likely to develop an agenda relating to that. By that I mean that even when the mentee has expressed no desire (or even a reluctance) to return to academic study, the mentor will still pursue this idea.

The mentor perceives expectation upon them, e.g. from a third party

Developing a personal agenda can happen when the mentor feels pressure to improve the results of the mentee, or 'improve' them in some way. This is possible where the mentoring is part of a scheme run in an organisation because business expectations (and therefore an agenda) are set. For example, the organisation may be using mentoring because it wants to develop talent, or deal with an individual's lack of progress or poor performance. Where the mentee is aware of these expectations from outside of the relationship (perhaps from HR or the mentee's manager), these must be discussed openly with all parties, including the mentee. That way, they can be discussed and incorporated, e.g. at the setting-out stage of the assignment.

Exercise

Spot a growing personal agenda

Use the following exercise to increase your awareness of any agendas you may have for your mentee, e.g. their behaviours, actions or results. It can help to write down your thoughts so that you can review them afterwards.

Step One

Think about your mentee's stated development themes and goals:

- What is your opinion about those?

- How would you feel if they didn't achieve them?
- What other themes or goals do you think they should have?

Step Two

Reflect on the previous two or three interactions you have had with your mentee (conversations, telephone calls, emails, etc.):

- Consider your 'attention and intention' when you are in conversation with them (Do the 'Notice your intention as you listen' exercise in Chapter 4 if that helps).
- How aware are you of a need to 'fix' or 'improve' your mentee?
- How do you feel when they change direction, e.g. by introducing new topics or goals?

Step Three (optional)

Where you have noticed an agenda present, e.g. 'I want them to take more risks' or 'I want them to be open to doing things differently', reflect on the following:

- How does your agenda affect your thoughts, feelings or behaviours?
- If you didn't have this agenda, what would be different?
- What have you decided to do?

Use the guiding principles to avoid building a personal agenda

When we create our own agenda for our mentee, e.g. become attached to them achieving certain results, we have moved away from guiding principles, such as:

- The responsibility for learning, progress and results ultimately rests with your mentee.
- Some results of mentoring can be identified or measured, while some results cannot. (This does not mean they are insignificant or less important, it simply means you are less aware of them.)

- Ultimately, what your mentee chooses to do, learn or ignore from the mentoring is not the mentor's business.

It's useful to return to these occasionally, to see whether you are forgetting any of them and straying off course as a result. For a summary of key principles and messages, see Chapter 7.

The subtle work of our familiar friend: the ego

While you become aware of your tendency to want them to see it your way or get them to understand something, sometimes you can find no clear logic for your behaviour. You might think their goals are great and their progress is good, but then in conversation you find that you interrupt them too often, or don't listen properly, or keep trying to 'fix' things for them.

You'll recall that our ego is a function of our mind (one that likes to control, be right, look smart, etc.). You may also have guessed that having a personal agenda for someone else often comes from a desire to know the answer, be perceived as having added value or simply wanting to be in charge. It is a natural tendency of the mind to also justify a need to do this, e.g. 'I know what they should do!' or 'Why can't they see this my way?'

If this sounds like you, please don't criticise yourself for doing this – that won't help either. Self-criticism, worry or concern is simply more to think about and your (unnecessary) thoughts move you away from a still and focused mind. Remember, when we stay focused on the present moment, the ego's influence upon us is much less because we literally think fewer thoughts.

Having a personal agenda for someone else often comes from a desire to know the answer

The ego's greatest enemy of all is the present moment.

Eckhart Tolle, author

During conversation: avoid an agenda by staying present

As previously, when we work to stay present to someone, we focus on them and what is being said or happening in the moment. When we are present, we think fewer thoughts and become more aware. We are literally more conscious (lucid) than when our minds are over-active in analysis or deep in foggy thought.

To practise and improve your tendency to stay present, take another look at the exercise 'Build better listening' in Chapter 4. Finally, remember that developing an ability to stay present in situations may seem difficult at first, but like a muscle that's used regularly, your tendency to do that will strengthen over time.

6.3 Pitfall Three: Allowing the idea of being a mentor to suggest superiority or prestige

This pitfall occurs when we confuse an emphasis or focus on the mentor (because we have something the mentee wants) with superiority. Where the mentor is perceived as having status somehow, such as a more senior role, this is an understandable pitfall of mentoring. Viewed literally, the mentor may feel personally superior or may feel they have a dominant advantage – perhaps more important or intelligent, etc. As a result they may treat the mentee as having less status in the relationship, perhaps speaking to them as if they are in some way naïve, or giving them instructions. The dynamic of the relationship may also shift towards feeling more like parent–child than one of equals, i.e. adult–adult.

Additionally, where a mentee's respect for the mentor may also indicate admiration, this is an easy trap for the mentor's ego, e.g. 'This person looks up to me, and I enjoy that.' While this will not automatically create an ineffective relationship, it does present the following risks:

- The mentee views their mentor as detached, less approachable or even aloof and this becomes a barrier to open communication.

- The mentee is less able to truly understand their mentor, e.g. what are the underlying principles he/she operates from; what really works for them?

- The potential benefits of a relationship based in equality are lost, e.g. an open exchange of ideas and views, increased disclosure (by either party) resulting in progress.

- The previous factors reduce the potential for high levels of engagement (by either party) in the relationship.

- The relationship never goes beyond the more superficial stages of set-up and pleasantries, and ends early.

The importance of self-awareness

This pitfall of superiority is a subtle one as it demands self-awareness from you as a mentor to spot both the tendency and the impact it is having upon your outlook and behaviour. By self-awareness, I literally mean awareness of yourself and how you think and feel. Features of self-awareness include:

- You have a clear and objective view of your strengths and weaknesses.

- You are able to understand what you think and feel in the present moment.

- You can judge your feelings in relation to situations, e.g. 'I've got too frustrated about this.'

- You understand your behavioural drivers ('I do this because. . .'). For example, 'I tend to over-check travel details before a big trip because when I'm sure everything is sorted it helps me relax.'

- You can predict your feelings, e.g. 'I won't enjoy that' or 'I would thrive in that situation.'

Awareness presents choice

Self-awareness is an important quality for us to develop, as it helps us make better behavioural choices in situations. When we are self-aware, we are more conscious of what we're doing and why we're doing that. This means we can make better choices in the moment and over time. Imagine that you're in a mentoring conversation and you are talking too much, perhaps you're over-explaining your ideas or giving too many examples. If you aren't aware you are doing that, you will simply continue and allow the potentially negative impact of that to occur. Perhaps your mentee begins to switch off, or is simply confused about the point of the conversation. However, when you notice – 'Ah, I'm talking too much' – you are more able to do something about it (such as relax, summarise your point and then ask the mentee a question). Over time you will reduce your tendency to talk too much and so become more effective in conversations.

Self-awareness is an important quality for us to develop, as it helps us make better behavioural choices in situations

A need to stay self-aware as your relationship develops

For any mentor, the pitfall of superiority can be fallen into quickly, or develop along with the relationship. For example, when you are asked to mentor someone, your responses might range from:

1. Well, that feels a bit daunting, I'm not sure I'm up to this.
2. That's an interesting challenge; I think I might really enjoy that.
3. Wow, that's flattering, I wonder why they chose me.
4. I've always wanted to mentor someone; I like the idea of someone 'looking up' to me.
5. That's great, it's about time my experience was recognised; anyone could learn a lot from me.

While responses 4 and 5 seem to indicate a perception of superiority from the outset, any of the above responses might develop into a feeling of superiority over time.

A need to maintain equality

As a mentor, you need to retain a sense of equality in the relationship, i.e. that you are no better or worse than your mentee, and that this is a relationship where both parties have equal ability to influence. Use the exercise below to review how much equality you perceive in a relationship.

Truth test

How equal are you?

Pick a relationship where you might assume to have more status by virtue of your position. That might range from someone on a lower grade in the workplace to someone who provides you with a service you pay for, such as cleaning your house, washing your car, or serving you food/drinks, etc. Use the following questions to examine the levels of equality in that relationship.

I can easily acknowledge a sense of 'sameness' with this person.

True ❏ **False** ❏

I would be comfortable disclosing information about myself with this person, e.g. discussing a mild personal concern/problem.

True ❏ **False** ❏

In a domestic setting, I would be very comfortable offering (and making) a cup of tea/coffee for this person.

True ❏ **False** ❏

I regard this person as having something to offer me, e.g. ideas or views I might be interested in.

True ❏ **False** ❏

If this person had a strongly held, different view about a situation to my own, I would reconsider my view and perhaps adapt it as a result.

True ❏ **False** ❏

These questions are simply to help provoke reflection and help you estimate the amount of equality you perceive in the relationship. For example, if your responses are mostly or all 'True', then it's likely you are perceiving levels of equality. If they are mostly 'False', then it is likely you perceive a different status in the relationship.

Use humility to help create a sense of equality

As a mentor, I encourage you to retain a sense of humility in relationship to the role as a way of avoiding a sense of superiority. Retaining a sense of humility as a mentor does not mean that you should put yourself in a 'lower' position to the person you are mentoring; humility is simply an opportunity to perceive yourself appropriately in the context of the relationship. For example, there is an element of privilege to be asked to mentor someone as you have the chance to be involved in your mentee's development in quite a personal way. So if the idea that being someone's mentor is something you might be appreciative of/ thankful for, then you're likely to have good access to the quality of humility. However, if you imagine that the mentee is lucky to have you, or that they should be grateful that you are spending time with them, this tends to indicate that you view yourself as superior in some way.

Humility is simply an opportunity to perceive yourself appropriately in the context of the relationship

How can you increase a sense of equality?

As you know, our perception of something creates our reality of it. For example, if you think scientists are full of amazing knowledge and have a fascinating way of viewing the world, then you will enjoy being around them. However, if you decide the same group of people are likely to intimidate, judge or view you as 'stupid', then you might not. Or if you imagine that your job is better (more important, more valuable, etc.) than one job but not as good as another, that might affect your perception when you meet people with those jobs. Imagine that you walk into a meeting room and a senior executive has brought along their personal assistant: you may locate yourself in a position of relative importance to those two people – such as 'below' the senior executive but 'above' the personal assistant. My logic is that where you may have 'placed' yourself in a perceived position of equality or inequality, you can shift your perception to be something different.

> *Change the way you look at things and the things you look at change.*
>
> Wayne W. Dyer

Of course, you may argue that other people or events make this happen, e.g. 'I am three pay grades higher than the personal assistant and there's nothing I can do about that.' While that may be factually correct, the fact shapes your perception only if you allow it to. Try this: can you think of any situation where you have felt 'less than equal' to someone where actually there might have been equality, e.g. a peer, friend, or complete stranger?

To further increase your self-awareness in relation to this topic, use the exercise below.

Exercise

How are you creating your perceptions of equality?

Think of three relationships that fall into the following perceived categories:

- where you feel there is equality in the relationship, e.g. of status, power and influence

---

- where you feel you have higher status or influence, e.g. you are more 'senior' in some way. You may have related facts that help you do that, e.g. I know more, have more experience, hold a more senior role, etc.

- where you feel you have less influence, e.g. you are less 'senior' in your own perception. Again, you may have facts that help you do that.

Next, consider each relationship in combination with the following questions:

In this relationship, what do you imagine that is true or not true that supports (justifies) your perception?

How does your view of your perceived seniority/equality/inequality shape your behaviours around this person?

If it would be of benefit to shift your perception, what would you have to believe? What impact would that have on your behaviour?

For each relationship it's likely that you will be so used to thinking and acting in certain ways around this person that it's possible to confuse 'what's familiar' with 'fact'. Please remember that you have decided your relative position at some point in the relationship and therefore logic indicates that you can change that decision.

6.4 Pitfall Four: Low levels of engagement

As an effective mentor, you aim to sustain good levels of engagement, both for yourself and as something you encourage in your mentee. Good levels of engagement are a pre-requisite for a successful relationship as they help both the mentor and the mentee to:

- be clear about and aligned with the aims of the mentoring activity

- feel motivated at the prospect of tackling the challenges involved

- sustain active effort even when things get difficult or arduous, e.g. 'to go the extra mile'.

What creates engagement?*

To help us understand what creates, reduces or prevents engagement, it's useful to break it down into component parts.

1. **The intellectual part**

   How we understand something, how clear we are about it and what our view/opinion is of that.

2. **The emotional part**

   Literally how we feel about doing something; the emotions that are being created by our thoughts/understanding.

3. **The enabling/'in action' part**

   What we are doing (the actions we are taking) in response to our understanding, views and feelings about something.

How engagement affects your responses

Imagine you are asked to mentor someone and are told very little about them or what they want to get from mentoring. Then you arrive at an initial meeting to wait for the mentee who doesn't show. When you finally make contact with them, they freely admit they hadn't read the email properly describing the need to confirm or rearrange the first meeting. Now you have:

a. **The intellectual part**

   You are unclear as to why you might want to support this person with mentoring; you may also have a view that the mentee has acted unprofessionally or even disrespectfully.

b. **The emotional part**

   Your feelings might range from fairly neutral ('these things happen') to feelings of annoyance ('I've been treated unprofessionally').

---

* Acknowledgement: Towers Watson (formerly Towers Perrin Consulting).

c. **The doing/acting part**

What you actually do (the acting part) will depend on your perspectives from (a) and (b). Perhaps you stay in a neutral position, e.g. agree to reschedule and decide to 'wait and see' before you judge your mentee's behaviour. Alternatively, where you view their behaviour as highly inappropriate or completely disrespectful, you may even refuse to meet them.

Alternatively, imagine that you are asked to mentor someone and are given a detailed brief about their situation and circumstances and what they want help with. You are told that they have requested to be mentored by you specifically as they have heard positive things about you from other people. You arrive at the initial meeting and the mentee doesn't show. When you make contact with them, they admit that their nerves had got the better of them at the prospect of meeting you in person. An hour before the scheduled meeting, they left a message with one of your team but you didn't get it. Now you have:

a. **The intellectual part**

You are clear as to what this person wants support with; you may also have a view that you are able to do that, e.g. as you recognise their lack of confidence.

b. **The emotional part**

Your feelings are likely to be more positive, e.g. 'I'm happy to overlook this' to 'I feel enthusiastic at the idea of working with this person.'

c. **The doing/acting part**

What you do as a result of (a) and (b) might vary from simply attending the next session as previously to arriving with a draft agenda and a pile of articles and information that you think might help them. This is engagement in action and will impact how you feel and how you act in relation to your mentee and the overall assignment.

Reduced levels of engagement: as a mentor

Where a mentor has low engagement about a mentoring relationship, while there are few sudden impacts there are potential consequences over time, such as:

- The mentor feels demotivated, e.g. 'This is a hassle' or 'I don't have the energy for this', which creates resistant behaviours, such as cancelling meetings at short notice.
- The mentor invests less tangible effort into the relationship, e.g. is less willing to provide practical help.
- In conversations with their mentee, their lack of engagement may reduce the quality of their attention or have them appear less 'sharp'.
- The mentor's tenacity is likely to be reduced, e.g. to tackle challenges or stay resourceful if things become difficult.
- The mentor is less likely to enjoy the experience of mentoring, i.e. as mentoring feels unimportant or a trial to them.

As a mentor, if you feel your motivation or engagement in an assignment is low, first you need to understand what is causing that. Some situations present more opportunity for improvement than others (as some issues can be solved more easily). Table 6.2 suggests potential solutions based on a range of different causes.

Reduced levels of engagement: From the mentee

Where your mentee has low levels of engagement, this is likely to impair both their attitude and actions related to the mentoring activity. The impact of reduced engagement in your mentee can include:

- They do not put additional effort into the mentoring, e.g. trying new ideas, changing their approach to situations, or tackling blocks or barriers to progress.
- They continue with the sessions despite viewing them as a 'waste of time' (which might make the mentor feel like that too).

Table 6.2 Dealing with low motivation as a mentor

Situation/Cause	Option/Solution	Observation
The mentor feels they have other pressures that outweigh the benefits of mentoring someone, e.g. 'I'm too busy with other priorities to make this important.'	✔ Understand if the situation is temporary, e.g. will things get better in time? ✔ Consider delaying mentoring activity or perhaps just reducing the mentor's active involvement, e.g. less frequent sessions, shorter meetings, etc. ✔ Explore the potential to reshape other priorities, to create more time to mentor. Where none exists, consider the impact of continuing with this reduced sense of motivation and engagement.	Consider whether it's appropriate to communicate the situation with your mentee or any scheme coordinator. For example, is there benefit in discussing the issue first? Sometimes this situation can reveal a useful perspective on the mentor's situation for the mentee, e.g. 'They're more senior than me and they are clearly overworked.'
The mentor is unclear as to the potential benefits for them, e.g. they don't think they will learn much, or enjoy doing it.	Increase your awareness of how mentoring benefits you, e.g. use reflection notes following meetings (What did I get from that? What did I enjoy about that?). Perform a review of the mentoring with the mentee to understand their perspective (see 'Review an assignment' in Appendix 3). Finally, decide whether what has become clear through the previous stages is sufficient to improve your perspective.	Sometimes there is value in just keeping going as the benefits of mentoring someone become more obvious over time – for example, as you gain increased skills during the conversation, or notice how the mentee is benefiting from your support. Talking to a third party can also help, e.g. discussing your concerns with someone you can trust.
The mentor's 'I can't be bothered' response is actually masking fear/unease (as they feel they lack the ability to be an effective mentor).	First understand what you need to do to reduce your unease, such as: ✔ increase knowledge or awareness of the process ✔ gain specific skills ✔ simply gain more experience (do more mentoring).	This is another situation where getting your own mentor can help, e.g. to obtain a view of mentoring from a mentee perspective in order to gain a clearer appreciation of what to make important – and what to relax about.

Situation/Cause	Option/Solution	Observation
The mentor decides their mentee lacks potential in some way, e.g. 'I just can't see them improving at all' or 'They're a bit of a no-hoper.'	Identify and then challenge your own view, for example: 1. What do I believe about them/their ability to progress? 2. Is that really true? (Can I know that for certain?) 3. What belief would I need to operate from in order to feel more positive about their potential? (Hint: try the exact opposite of the belief from No. 1.) 4. If I operated from this new belief, what would be different? 5. What have I decided to do?	This is important to deal with as this issue can have a surprisingly negative impact for the mentee, for example: ✔ Your view of their poor potential may communicate through your behaviour or demeanour. ✔ As their mentor, your view is potentially a strong influence upon them. ✔ Your belief that they lack potential might become something that they also buy into (or accept).
You are part of an organisational scheme and your involvement as a mentor is mandatory (rather than optional). You are not enthusiastic about mentoring someone and are resistant to doing that.	Understand more about what is causing your specific reluctance. For example: ✔ Are you simply annoyed at being put in this position? ✔ Are you concerned that you won't make a good mentor? ✔ Do you lack enough information about mentoring to judge how you might really feel about it? (Check the previous examples in this table for a relevant perspective that might apply to you.)	Once you understand specifically what is causing your resistance, you can make a more informed decision of what's best for you and your mentee. For example, where you have the tendency to resist being instructed/made to do something, perhaps check out the 'Approval or control?' exercise in Chapter 3.

As a mentor, while you are happy to meet someone and discuss their situations, you are not convinced in the potential of mentoring, i.e. don't believe that mentoring makes a difference to anyone.	Get focused. Follow the process steps in Chapter 5, e.g. set expectations and a sense of routine and structure. Let the process prove itself, e.g. as you reflect and review progress. Decide to keep an open mind until you've had enough sessions to judge objectively, e.g. 4–6 mentoring sessions/conversations. Move to stage four of the Mentor's process 'Set down' (again in Chapter 5). After the review point, reflect to help you decide and negotiate the best way forward with your mentee, i.e. continue or complete the relationship.	This issue can present unexpected gifts. When someone who has been initially cynical of something becomes convinced, they often become an advocate/champion of it. This is because the process they have been through to change their mind has proven something beyond their initial doubts of it.
The mentor is suffering generally from a lack of de-motivation, or low morale and this is impacting every area of what they do.	Again, there is a need to: ✔ raise your awareness of what the issue actually is (symptoms, cause and impact) ✔ understand your options for a way forward ✔ understand your criteria for making a decision, e.g. a need to prioritise your health, enjoyment or learning ✔ choose the best option(s) available to you ✔ act on that (and get support to do so if appropriate).	This seems the most obvious situation to consider pausing or ending your mentoring activity. Your decision must evaluate the nature of your lowered motivation and also the impact this is having on your mentee. This may range from 'mild de-motivation' to 'extreme negativity'. As a mentor, your commitment to the progress of your mentee requires you to withdraw where you feel you are having a limiting or negative impact upon that.

- They do not connect to the idea of 'the mentor has something that I need' and so do not pursue or discover that.
- They blame the mentor for their lack of progress (rather than stay responsible for their own learning).
- They don't benefit from the opportunity of mentoring, e.g. by making progress in their situations or experiencing personal growth.
- They blame themselves for their lack of progress, e.g. 'I'm a hopeless case'.
- Their self-esteem or confidence is actually reduced by the experience, rather than grown by it.

Stay objective and have an intention to assist

Again, it is important to understand what is causing your mentee's apparent low engagement before responding to it. It's also critical to stay objective, by which I mean assess the facts, rather than your interpretation of the facts. For example, it may be factual to observe that your mentee does not act upon the majority of the actions they commit to during sessions. However, it is an exaggeration to say 'they don't keep any of them' and subjective to say 'it's because they are lazy'. It is also important to maintain your intention to provide appropriate assistance, rather than dwelling on your own feelings about the matter. Perhaps the idea of 'laziness' is one that you have strong views about and your perspective may be coloured by that. Remember also your principle of 'benevolence' towards the individual, to help you remain balanced in the situation.

It is important to understand what is causing your mentee's apparent low engagement before responding to it

Understanding present insight

If you aren't clear what is causing your mentee's apparent low engagement, then an objective (facts-based) conversation based on supportive intentions about that is a good place to start. For example, perhaps they don't say much during conversations with you, or act upon the advice and ideas you are giving them. Here's a less objective response which indicates a less supportive intention:

- You decide their not following up on actions means they are not engaged, so you need to 'tackle' what you see as a definite issue. So you give them 'feedback' and assert your position, e.g. 'You're clearly not engaged in this and I'm keen not to waste each other's time'.

Your subjectivity comes from the fact that you have a) decided they are not engaged and that b) they are aware of it. The 'let's not waste each other's time' comment suggests lack of positive intention or perhaps commitment; that you view the apparent lack of progress as a barrier or block unworthy of tackling: 'let's not bother', 'let's give up', etc. Positioning the situation like this may also create feelings of defensiveness, or 'being told off', in the mentee. It is less likely to encourage comfort and open disclosure from them with this approach, e.g. 'Thanks, I'm glad you've raised this ... '

Here's a more objective response which expresses an intention to help:

- You decide that 'something isn't working' e.g. they are quiet, not making obvious progress, etc. and need to understand more so that you can help them (if that's appropriate). So you offer supportive observations and ask for their view, e.g. 'Here's what I'm noticing and here's what I think might be the potential impact of that for you', followed by 'Is that fair? How do you see this?'

Take care to offer objective observations, e.g. 'I notice you don't speak much in conversations' or 'I'm offering you lots of ideas and advice but I'm not sure that you are benefiting from that'. While this may still be uncomfortable for the mentee to hear, they are likely to be more able to respond, as they are less 'judged' or criticised in your observations. You are also demonstrating a willingness to be wrong. ('Is that fair? How do you see this?')

Once you understand a little more about the situation, you can decide the best way to respond to it, in collaboration with your mentee. Table 6.3 highlights some symptoms, causes and potential responses.

6.5 Pitfall Five: Avoiding dependency/mutual dependency

Any one-on-one relationship presents the potential for either party (or both parties) to become dependent on each other. By becoming dependent, I mean that one party feels a sense of reliance on the other for something and would feel a sense of loss (or being uncomfortable) at the idea of not having it. It is important that you and your mentee remain independent of each other to enable the benefits of mentoring to be realised: that they become more empowered and equipped to face future challenges, etc.

Dependency can often occur where there is a stated intention of support; perhaps for a mentee 'being helped' creates a feeling of 'I need help'. Alternatively, as a mentor's support is clearly appreciated by the mentee, the mentor translates that to a sense of 'I am needed'. Here are some examples of that:

- A mentee can become dependent on their mentor:
  - for the regular praise and encouragement they get from the mentor, which gives them a temporary sense of increased self-esteem or confidence
  - to help them make decisions and stay clear and committed to those (as they rely on you to help them to decide what to do)
  - for the temporary 'feel-good' factor following conversations, e.g. 'They lighten my load, they're like mini therapy sessions and without them I'd go nuts.'

Table 6.3 Dealing with a mentee's low engagement

Situation/Cause	Option/Solution	Observation
During your conversations, your mentee consistently decides to complete actions after sessions but then does not. When you enquire, you discover that procrastination is a core issue for them and this isn't just related to the mentoring activity.	This is a 'barrier' or 'block' they need your help to overcome. Now you are both aware of their tendency, you provide 'appropriate assistance', e.g. facilitate their thinking, offer ideas, advice, etc.	Remember, what the mentee does or does not do outside of sessions is not your business. This can help you detach emotionally from the situation, and so not get frustrated, disappointed, etc.
The mentee appears disinterested during your conversations, and lacks motivation to improve the sessions. When you explore the behaviour, they explain that they think you're not the best mentor for them as your background isn't what they were looking for.	Use the principle of 'the mentor has something that the mentee needs' to understand the validity of their view. ✔ Return to the areas they want support with, or to develop in. ✔ Share your own ideas of what they need to learn or need assistance with. ✔ Use this joint enquiry to help them decide what they want to do.	Whatever arises from the joint enquiry will have a positive impact on the situation, e.g. they decide to re-engage with the relationship, or you both complete the relationship and are free to work with other people. Try not to make this personal/about you – stay objective and dispassionate. Use reflection notes to process your own thoughts/feelings if appropriate, or the 'Approval or control?' exercise in Chapter 3.
The mentee constantly rates mentoring-related activities as secondary or less important to other things, shows up late, leaves early, reschedules at short notice, etc. During enquiry, they appear unaware that they do this, e.g. these behaviours feel pretty normal for them. They give the impression they don't view it as a major issue.	This can be an opportunity to assist in removing a block or barrier they are unaware of, for example: ✔ a need to develop better standards of efficiency or personal organisation ✔ a need to develop higher levels of self-discipline ✔ a need to create positive professional impressions. Make requests for them to demonstrate respect for your time and monitor the situation.	Again, don't take this personally (stay objective and dispassionate). Remember, what drives any relationship that endures over time is our on-going commitment to it. Sometimes your commitment means disappointing that person, perhaps by: ✔ leaving a session if they are late ✔ suspending your mentoring conversations for a while (if their behaviour doesn't improve) ✔ in extreme cases, completing the active part of the relationship.

- A mentor can become dependent on their mentee:
  - when they might enjoy the feeling of being 'needed' or valued by someone else, where that matches a need that they have to feel wanted, valued, special, etc.
  - when the relationship helps them boost a professional or personal profile they feel they need, e.g. being a mentor gives them better status in their workplace
  - when the mentor enjoys the level of influence they have on the mentee and that develops into more of a 'parenting' or controlling role.
- The mentor and mentee can become dependent on each other (mutual dependency):
  - when both parties become reliant on the relationship and would feel a sense of real loss without it: 'Where would we be without these sessions?'
  - when items from the previous lists are combined, such as, 'They say they need my help and knowing that gives me confidence outside of the sessions'
  - where the routine of meeting up for conversations is habit forming and the need to stop doing that introduces change and creates mutual discomfort.

Noticing dependency upon you as mentor

As a mentor, it helps to recognise signs and symptoms of dependency so that you can decide the best response to that. Table 6.4 outlines situations of dependency from a mentee, to help your thinking.

Noticing dependency in yourself as mentor

Spotting that as a mentor you have become dependent on the mentoring relationship in some way can be more tricky, simply because we are less likely to notice it as a problem (because it won't feel like one). Also, we tend to judge other people on their behaviours, yet judge ourselves on our intention. This means that if we intend to be supportive and provide assistance, we may judge a controlling behaviour as 'just trying to help'.

Table 6.4 Signs and symptoms of dependency in a mentee

Indication that mentee has dependency	Potential responses
The mentee regularly delays making decisions, e.g. 'I said I couldn't give them an answer until I've spoken to you.' The mentee appears to consistently view the mentor's ideas and opinions as automatically better, or more important than their own, e.g. 'If that's what you think, then that's what I'll do.'	This signals a need for the mentor to raise the topic sensitively with the mentee, as follows: 1. Confirm the relevant principle, in this case a need for the conversations to enable the mentee to make decisions themselves, or feel more empowered generally. 2. Offer observations and examples ('Here's what I'm seeing') before exploring how the mentee views the situation ('How do you see this?'). 3. Discuss the options for a way forward and agree actions from those.
Where your agreed schedule is once every 6–8 weeks, the mentee asks for more frequent sessions or several short-notice sessions, e.g. 'I've got something I really need your input on.'	Meeting more frequently or at short notice to offer support during a particular situation does not necessarily indicate dependency. In some situations, you may decide that it is totally appropriate. However, if you feel that the mentee is becoming too reliant upon your involvement, perhaps use the three-step sequence above to increase awareness of the issue and shape change.
Over time, the nature of your conversations changes from having clear links to the development themes to perhaps discussing more detailed, everyday topics. You begin to feel as though the conversations are more problem solving in nature or alternatively that the mentee appears to need your input on 'anything and everything'.	This may be dependency as the mentee begins to portray you in the role of 'friendly manager'. However, it may be a simple need to refocus on the mentee's development themes or objectives of the relationship. Alternatively, this may be a situation co-created by the mentor, as they have also encouraged the conversation into more 'everyday chat'. Again, the previous three-step process from the first example might be useful for you.

Again, where we maintain self-awareness we are more likely to notice our increased dependency on the relationship over time. As a mentor you can maintain your self-awareness by perhaps writing reflection notes, or talking your mentoring relationship through with someone you can trust. The following questions could be used either to prompt conversation with someone or as prompts for a reflection note:

- What am I getting from this relationship, e.g. benefits, things I enjoy, etc.?
- How would I feel if those things were withdrawn or were not a feature of the relationship?
- How would I feel if the relationship ended, perhaps because my mentee requested that?

We tend to judge other people on their behaviours, yet judge ourselves on our intention

Only you can decide whether your answers feel balanced and in proportion to the relationship. Please remember, if you really enjoy the conversations because they are intellectually stimulating and you'd be disappointed if they were cut short – that's completely normal and healthy. However, if you suspect that you are keeping conversations going for a more egoic related reason (they make you feel liked, needed, flattered, admired, powerful etc.), that signals something to look at.

Table 6.5 illustrates different ways in which a mentor can become overly reliant on the interactions/relationship with a mentee and what is needed in each case.

Noticing mutual dependency

Mutual dependency may combine any of the previous factors, e.g. 'This is their dependency and this is mine.' As mentor, where you notice separate (unrelated) dependencies, use the previous examples to help you decide how to respond to each one.

Table 6.5 Signs and symptoms of dependency in a mentor

Indication that mentor has dependency	Observation
The mentor recognises their mentoring sessions are something they rely on for enjoyment, fun or a 'break in the monotony'. Where sessions need to be rescheduled, they are extremely disappointed. At the prospect of the sessions ending, they experience feelings of despondency or even despair.	While this situation doesn't automatically impair the success of a relationship, it easily might. Perhaps the mentee picks up on a sense of 'my mentor needs something from me' or feels relied upon somehow. The mentor needs to address the greater issue in the situation, namely that their surrounding situation feels like something they want a break from.
The mentor sustains their self-confidence or self-esteem through the relationship, e.g. they feel their mentee is the only person who really appreciates them. When another person or event threatens to lower their confidence or self-esteem, they remind themselves, 'Well my mentee thinks I'm great, they really value what I do.'	Again, a mentee may pick up on a sense of need from the mentor, e.g. for compliments or reassurances. The mentor becomes a less effective role model, as they appear to need the approval of others to function effectively. Here the mentor needs to build their self-esteem. First they need to understand what factors are causing their lowered self-esteem, e.g. people, situations, thoughts or beliefs. They then need to take action, to assert their ability to influence the situation, or change their limiting beliefs.
The mentor views their relationship with their mentee as the only relationship they have where they can be open, be themselves, really relax and be accepted. In other relationships they feel unable to speak their thoughts plainly and simply, as they fear judgement or disapproval. The idea of the relationship ending brings feelings of impending loss or even anxiety.	The mentor needs to reflect upon what they have done that has cultivated such an open, positive relationship. They can then use the same principles to foster similar relationships with others. For example, as they realise they assumed non-judgement or positive judgement from the outset, they were comfortable sharing more of their authentic views and feelings.

Alternatively, mutual dependency may combine dependencies you have in common, such as relying on the sessions for their fun factor or being able to get away from the daily grind. Where these elements are not balanced by more progressive features of the relationship, such as the mentee's growth and learning, or their being encouraged to tackle challenges and obstacles, then the potential of the mentoring has been diluted.

Use Table 6.6 to review or respond to symptoms of mutual dependency.

Dependency: a potential to invent a problem

As a mentor, the pitfall of dependency is one you need to stay aware of and yet not become distracted by. Asking the mentee to assist in monitoring the potential issue isn't helpful. Imagine the conversation, 'Hey, how are we doing with the potential issue of mutual dependency do you think?' – it would create a strange tone and emphasis to the relationship. Also, you can distract or waste time looking for issues that are not there instead of focusing on positive topics, such as the mentee's progress.

I recommend you combine the potential issue of dependency with your occasional reflections, perhaps using the questions below (write notes, or simply read them through) to prompt thought:

- What are the benefits/enjoyable aspects of our sessions/ relationship?
- If these benefits/enjoyable aspects were not present, how would that affect the progress of my mentee?
- How would I feel if the relationship ended?
- How do I think my mentee might feel if the relationship ended?
- How independent are we of each other within the relationship?

Finally, you might also reflect on the mentoring principles, occasionally, to ensure they still feel present in the relationship.

Table 6.6 Mutual dependence in the mentor–mentee relationship

Indication mentor and mentee are mutually dependent	Potential responses
Mentoring conversations become a place to offload where you both share problems, moan, complain, express negative emotions, etc. Your mentee's progress seems limited, either in relation to their initial goals/development themes or in the situations they complain about. As mentor, you have lost a sense of the mentor role, e.g. providing appropriate assistance, or supporting learning and growth.	The approach depends on how prevalent the issue has become. For example, if the tendency to offload is mild yet noticeable, the mentor is able to: ✔ revisit the mentor principles to identify those that they need to act from (and do that) ✔ use reflection notes to increase self-awareness and progressive choice, e.g. 'How appropriate was the way I helped during that session?' ✔ increase their use of structure and process to encourage a constructive approach, e.g. 'Let's confirm what you need help to do, or look at ways to overcome apparent obstacles.' ✔ Where the issue is more prevalent, or doesn't respond to the above methods, a more open conversation with the mentee is needed, e.g. 'Here's what I notice we are both doing, and here's the issue with that.'
Your mentoring relationship feels enjoyably sociable, e.g. you meet up, have fun, swap updates and stories, often with the intention of entertaining each other. As mentor, you have lost a sense of your role, e.g. of having something the mentee wants (in order to make progress). You have let any sense of structure go, as it feels misaligned to the nature of the conversation. You both acknowledge how much you look forward to sessions, simply because they are so much fun. If the relationship were to end, you would both regret the loss of such a great friendship.	The choice here should be made as to what is best for your mentee. Your options include: 1. Discontinue as their mentor, continue as their friend. 2. Use the available structure, principles and process to recover the potential benefits of a mentor relationship. 3. Complete the relationship (and consider the option of a different mentor). Your relationship has become friendship, so an open conversation is appropriate, to share views, understand what seems important and decide the way forward.

Chapter summary

Any relationship with a mentee brings its challenges and pitfalls that can lessen both the quality and success of the relationship. These pitfalls include:

- placing yourself under too much pressure
- having a personal agenda (strategising)
- allowing the idea of being a mentor to suggest superiority or prestige
- low levels of engagement
- avoiding dependency/mutual dependency.

As a mentor, by staying aware of those potential pitfalls, you can avoid them or respond constructively as they arise. As with any potential risk, you need a balanced approach to that (to avoid creating an issue where none actually exists). For example, check back over the list of pitfalls occasionally, or use reflection techniques to maintain your self-awareness. Where you are comfortable that you operate from the main mentor principles fairly consistently, it is likely that you are naturally avoiding the major pitfalls.

Chapter

7

Honesty is the first chapter in the book of wisdom.

Thomas Jefferson, third President of the USA

Summary and closing thoughts

In this chapter:

- A summary of key definitions, messages and principles of mentoring.
- Consolidate your current position as you begin or continue to mentor others.
- Decide on the ideas or themes that you want to take forward.

Summary of key messages

Let's look at the main messages from the book, to help you review and reflect on them. You may also find this section a useful place to return to later to be reminded of ideas or find signposts that indicate where to find key topics and information.

From Chapter 1

Mentoring is defined by the nature and intention of a relationship, rather than the specific behaviours within it, such as:

- A mentor's aim is to support the learning, development and progress of another person (their mentee).
- They use a range of methods to provide support, such as giving information, advice and practical assistance.
- They balance their involvement in a way that empowers the mentee, for example:

- sometimes they are required to be a 'wise guide' and draw upon their own experiences to offer insight and advice

- sometimes they might offer to 'do' something for someone else, e.g. make an introduction, or review a document

- sometimes the mentor adopts a more detached posture, acting as a facilitator who helps the mentee to think and decide for themselves.

While a mentor has unique attributes that define the role, this role is familiar to us and we can identify people we feel are or have been a mentor to us. Additionally, we regularly perform this role for others, often without appreciating that.

From Chapter 2

An active mentor relationship has typical attributes that work together to create a foundation for success.

- The mentor is providing assistance over a period of time, during which the mentee has a sense of purpose, e.g. to gain something, to develop at something, etc. This period of time can also be thought of as a 'quest' involving worthwhile challenges that must be overcome.

- The mentor has something the mentee needs, such as:

  - knowledge, experience and/or wisdom, which is relevant to the mentee's purpose or objectives

  - resources that the mentee might benefit from, such as professional connections, or access to information or services

  - personal qualities that can assist and sustain the mentee, e.g. an objective outlook, a positive/objective disposition or simply kindness and warmth.

- The relationship is an effective harmony of benevolence and respect. The mentor feels a sense of benevolence towards the mentee that helps sustain their commitment to their progress. The mentee respects the mentor and so is open to be influenced by them. While the mentee may also feel benevolence towards the mentor, and the mentor respects the mentee, the effectiveness of the relationship does not rely upon that.

From Chapter 3

As you mentor someone else, your effective choices or responses are supported by a set of guiding principles, namely:

1. Your relationship is one of equality and yet has a natural bias/emphasis (upon the mentor).
2. The responsibility for learning, progress and results ultimately rests with your mentee.
3. Mentoring is collaboration between you, your mentee and 'everyday life'.
4. Ultimately, what your mentee chooses to do, learn or ignore from the mentoring is not the mentor's business.
5. Some results of mentoring can be identified or measured, while some results cannot. (This does not mean they are insignificant or less important, it simply means you are less aware of them.)

From Chapter 4

Mentors come in different shapes and guises and yet share the same tendencies and abilities, namely:

- they are able to connect through effective listening
- they build a relationship of engagement and trust
- they help the mentee to maintain an effective focus, i.e. on what they need to do to maintain progress
- they help the mentee overcome false limits, roadblocks or barriers to progress. These may be internal barriers (such as limiting beliefs) or barriers relating to circumstance (such as needing to get connected to a group of people who can help them)
- they help someone grow, learn and develop.

From Chapter 5

An active mentor relationship (or assignment) is supported by the idea of a process or journey, i.e. an experience with a beginning, middle and end. The stages, or milestones, along the journey are illustrated in Figure 5.1.

Figure 5.1 The Mentor Map

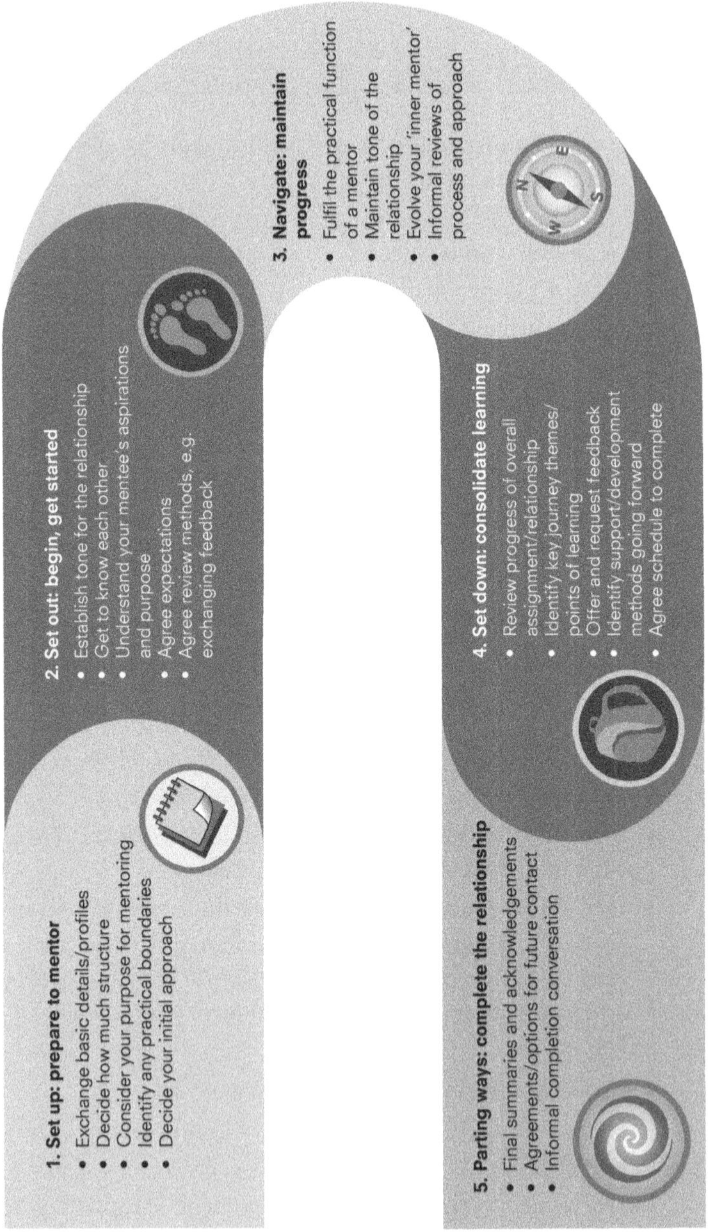

1. Set up: prepare to mentor
- Exchange basic details/profiles
- Decide how much structure
- Consider your purpose for mentoring
- Identify any practical boundaries
- Decide your initial approach

2. Set out: begin, get started
- Establish tone for the relationship
- Get to know each other
- Understand your mentee's aspirations and purpose
- Agree expectations
- Agree review methods, e.g. exchanging feedback

3. Navigate: maintain progress
- Fulfil the practical function of a mentor
- Maintain tone of the relationship
- Evolve your 'inner mentor'
- Informal reviews of process and approach

4. Set down: consolidate learning
- Review progress of overall assignment/relationship
- Identify key journey themes/points of learning
- Offer and request feedback
- Identify support/development methods going forward
- Agree schedule to complete

5. Parting ways: complete the relationship
- Final summaries and acknowledgements
- Agreements/options for future contact
- Informal completion conversation

From Chapter 6

During the journey of any mentor, there are pitfalls (or risks) that the mentor must avoid along the way, namely:

1. Placing yourself under too much pressure.

2. Having a personal agenda (strategising).

3. Allowing the idea of being a mentor to suggest superiority or prestige.

4. Low levels of engagement.

5. Avoiding dependency/mutual dependency.

By staying aware of these potential pitfalls, you can avoid them or respond constructively as they arise. As with any potential risk, you need a balanced approach (to avoid creating an issue where none actually exists). It's a good idea to check back over the list of pitfalls occasionally, or use reflection techniques to maintain your self-awareness.

Exercise

Consolidate your learning

Use the following sequence to understand where you are now, in relation to the previous ideas. Writing brief notes can help you to clarify and prioritise your thoughts.

1 First, let's understand your current perspectives, so having reviewed the previous summary of key messages:

- Which ideas or principles seem most important to you right now?

- How do you intend to use or apply those ideas?

- What do you expect to be the benefits of using them?

2 Next, it's also helpful to understand where reading the book has revealed or strengthened your ideas as a mentor. Again, thinking of the summary of key messages:

- What do you not like or what do you disagree with?

- Why do you disagree, i.e. what do you believe instead?

- How does your belief support you as a mentor?

▶

3 Now begin to create a forward focus that will help sustain and continue your development. Please note that you need only a few ideas to do this – the idea is simply to help you maintain an engagement to improve. Consider what you are still interested in or would like to be better at. For example:

- What would you like to know more about? (Information/knowledge.)
- What would you like to learn? (To integrate knowledge with awareness.)
- What would you like to be able to do even better? (To develop skills and abilities.)

4 Create a plan for action. Write down a list of actions or activities that would help you to make progress with your mentoring. Again, keep this simple, practical and achievable (to support yourself to succeed). For example:

- read one of the recommended books
- check out the Online Toolkit to see what you want to use
- have a look back through the exercises and try a few.

5 Finally, support yourself to achieve success with your actions. Review what you have decided you want (more awareness, ability, etc.) and also the actions you listed. Use the questions below to strengthen your plan:

- What might stop you completing the actions? (What are your potential barriers to progress?)
- What do you need to do to eliminate, overcome or simply ignore these barriers?
- Who can help or support you to achieve your plan?

Closing thoughts

Being a mentor for someone requires us to gather what we have experienced, what we have learned and what we are able to do, then consolidate that into suitably wrapped parcels to offer them. For a mentee, the gifts of being mentored include practical assistance, learning, growth and personal support that confirms that they are both valuable and valued. When you recall how your own mentors have made you feel about yourself, you connect with the potential contribution you can make as a mentor for others. Of course, as you develop your ability as a mentor, you are encouraged to appreciate your wealth of experience, insight and learning and that can be an additional and unexpected gain for a mentor.

I hope you have benefited from the ideas in this book and that they continue to support you over time. Please feel able to return to them occasionally to confirm and refresh your viewpoints, perhaps as questions or challenges arise. Remember that the Online Toolbox is available to assist you at starrconsulting.co.uk In the meantime, enjoy your own journey to liberate your 'inner mentor'. As Mahatma Gandhi said: 'The best way to find yourself is to lose yourself in the service of others.'

What did you think of this book?

We're really keen to hear from you about this book, so that we can make our publishing even better.

Please log on to the following website and leave us your feedback.

It will only take a few minutes and your thoughts are invaluable to us.

www.pearsoned.co.uk/bookfeedback

Appendix 1
Options for Session Two

Agenda A – Relationship emphasis

Ref.	Item	Approx. timing	Guidance
1.0	**Build the mentor's understanding of the mentee** The mentor 'interviews' the mentee to learn more of their background, current situation and preferences. For example: • So tell me more about how you come to be in this role and situation? • I'm interested to understand more about the work you do now. What are the challenges in that? • Can you describe what you want for the future, e.g. in your career or for your personal life? (To understand their aspirations)	20 min.	Rather than follow my topics and questions exactly, be willing to stay with what comes up and what you're genuinely interested in. That could be anything from their choice of career to their choice of football team.

▶

Ref.	Item	Approx. timing	Guidance
2.0	**Build the mentee's understanding of the mentor** • The mentee 'interviews' the mentor to learn more of their background, current situation and preferences. The mentee can use the previous agenda topics or simply interview the mentor according to their real interests and preferences.	20 min.	As mentor, this is an opportunity for you to display openness and trust, e.g. in the amount of disclosure you are comfortable with. Balance this with a need to be appropriate/stay relevant.
3.0	**Discuss and agree relationship principles** Use the following to confirm or agree how you will work together: • Responsibility for learning rests with the mentee (as the mentor stays 'committed and unattached'). • Mentoring is a collaboration between mentor, mentee and 'everyday life' (so there's a need to stay focused on outcomes while being adaptable to change). • What the mentee chooses to do, learn or ignore from the mentoring conversations is not the mentor's business (as they are not 'managing' but mentoring).	10 min.	Keep the tone of these light, e.g. 'This might or might not crop up' or 'For me what that means is simply ...'

Ref.	Item	Approx. timing	Guidance
4.0	**Create conversation on a key theme or topic** Take one of the mentee's development themes and discuss that, for example: • What interests you around this topic? • What objectives or goals do you have? • What are your (the mentor's) thoughts and experiences that may be relevant? (Consider also whether other assistance might be appropriate.)	30 min.	Check out 'Hints and tips: in conversation with your mentee 1 and 2' in Chapter 5.1.
5.0	**Mentee summarises and creates a sense of the way forward** The mentee gives an overview of where they are following the conversation and also how they want to take things forward, for example: • Here's what I think I've got from this. • Here's what I think I need to focus on or get done (commit to actions if appropriate). • Here's what might stop me (and here's how I intend to tackle that).	10 min.	As mentor you can naturally add to the summary and remember: • they need to engage with, and be empowered by, this process • what they do as a result of the conversation is something you must stay objective about • you are their mentor – not their manager.

Agenda B – Goal and task emphasis

Ref.	Item	Approx. timing	Guidance
1.0	**Build understanding: mentee's themes** The mentor 'interviews' the mentee to focus more directly on their objectives and development themes. For example: • Let's look more closely at what you want to get from this in terms of areas you want to develop or grow in. • Can you describe what you want for the future, e.g. in your career or for your personal life (understand their aspirations)? • What do you see as potential blocks or barriers to your progress, e.g. current challenges, gaps in knowledge or skills?	30 min.	Rather than follow my topics and questions exactly, be willing to stay with what comes up and follow your own instincts, e.g. 'Do they mean leadership or are they simply referring to a confident management style?'
2.0	**Focus on a topic or theme (1)** Take an initial topic or theme and create conversation around that theme, for example: • What would you like to focus on first? • I'm thinking we might talk about this one first – how does that sound? • Okay, let's talk about this one.	20 min.	Remember the conversation has a gentle bias on what you can add, e.g. by sharing your experience and wisdom.

3.0	**Focus on a topic or theme (2)** As on the previous page, take a second topic or theme and create conversation around that theme.	20 min.	Note: You might not have time for this second topic as the first topic may overrun during detailed discussion/ enquiry.
4.0	**Mentee summarises and creates a sense of the way forward** The mentee gives an overview of where they are following the conversation and also how they want to take things forward, for example: • Here's what I think I've got from this. • Here's what I think I need to focus on or get done (commit to actions if appropriate). • Here's what might stop me (and here's how I intend to tackle that).	10 min.	As mentor you can add to this, but please remember: ✔ they need to engage with, and be empowered by, this process ✔ what they do as a result of the conversation is something you must stay objective about ✔ you are their mentor – not their manager.
5.0	**Check expectations/ effectiveness** Discuss whether the conversation has seemed appropriate in style and approach to meet the mentee's needs, for example: • How much is this meeting your needs? • What else might we be missing? • What might we do more of/ less of next time?	10 min.	Here we review the approach or format during sessions, and also focus indirectly on the relationship, checking that the mentee is happy, reassuring them of flexibility, etc.

Appendix 2
Schedule and nature of a mentor's involvement

Example 1. An organised company scheme	Observations
The scheme coordinator matches you to a member of the company's identified talent, Alison, an engineer fresh into her first management position. You are asked to provide mentoring support for a term of 12 months and given a half-day 'Introduction to Mentoring' class, where you learn principles of mentoring, the process, approach, dos/don'ts, etc. Alison attends a similar half-day session to help her get the most from the experience, e.g. what she can expect from her mentor and what will be expected from her.	The scheme coordinator will normally be more involved during the set-up phase, then take a back seat, though be available to handle any issues that may arise.
Alison is a new manager who eventually wants to progress to a more general manager role (and move away from technical engineering involvement). Her goals are to develop her leadership style, personal impact and delegation skills. Your first three meetings are monthly, then afterwards every 6–8 weeks. As mentor, you add value through general discussion, e.g. of Alison's day-to-day situations and also sharing your own stories, insights and beliefs. You make observations and provide constructive feedback where appropriate. The conversations are broad ranging and sometimes challenging, e.g. as Alison asks unexpected questions or for examples to illustrate your beliefs. Sometimes you recommend books, YouTube videos, TED talks, etc. Alison keeps her own notes, arranges the agreed schedule of meetings and takes responsibility for any follow-up.	The coordinator may also encourage more formal review and evaluation methods, e.g. conduct evaluation interviews, send electronic questionnaires, etc. Alternatively, they may be comfortable with informal methods, e.g. ask you and the mentee for anecdotal feedback.
You both review the process informally throughout the year, e.g. what's working, what's not working? Alison reports that what she values most is your supportive style and that she feels she can bring anything into the conversation and knows you'll offer a view. After the agreed duration of 12 months, the assignment completes with an informal review and Alison notifies the coordinator of the scheme. The coordinator of the scheme contacts you for a final update, e.g. 'How did this go?', 'What else might be needed?'	

Example 2. You are a pro-active volunteer	Observation
You approach your local university to offer your time as a mentor as part of a scheme you've heard they offer to students. After a chat over the telephone, you complete a form detailing your career history and life experiences. You are assigned a mature student called Fiona, who is studying business management to help her start a delicatessen and coffee shop locally. While you currently help run your family's haulage business, you previously managed a busy high-street restaurant and can see potential links to her situation.	This is a less structured assignment that offers creative potential but also risk, e.g. that you try to help with something inappropriate.
You visit the university and meet the scheme coordinator, who explains the modest expectations upon you and broadly describes your mentee, Fiona. You are asked to provide a minimum of six hour-long sessions over the academic term, potentially on the university campus or at your place of work. Fiona has also been briefed and asked to arrange location and dates of meetings. You have an initial chat with Fiona on the telephone and agree to meet at your office.	When you operate from the principle that you have something the mentee wants, then you are more likely to identify this. This requires that you question the flow of the conversations, e.g. what help the mentee says they need.
You find that Fiona is naturally very focused on the processes of running a business, e.g. stock-control methods, pricing, financial forecasting, etc. These are areas that she says she wants help with, but you see few links with your own experience or core skills. Fiona also explains that she wants to have an environmentally friendly eco theme, which includes educating the customers on the global issues related to food production. You sense that some of Fiona's messages may wander into 'lecturing' and wonder how that will translate to the customer's experience. After running a restaurant yourself, you know that how the customer feels about what you do is a priority, e.g. as word of mouth spreads.	This relationship develops elements of an unlikely friendship and is mutually enjoyable because of that.
In your initial sessions you notice how engaged and knowledgeable Fiona is on financial modelling and environmental research. The link to you having something to offer still isn't clear, so you gently explain that these aren't topics you can help with, and also they are areas she appears very able to take forward. However, the topic of the customer's experience is something you feel you can help her develop more fully as something key to the success of her business. Fiona leaves the session unsure, then later contacts you to say she's realised that actually this is something that she would like to work on.	
You suggest that your following meetings are in a series of different food and drink outlets, where you can observe and discuss what works and what doesn't. You offer your own ideas to add to her list and buy her a book on transforming customer service. Fiona decides to adopt some of the creative ideas in the book.	
After six sessions, you both decide to continue the meetings to support the opening of the deli and café. Fiona keeps a learning diary, e.g. writes a note at the end of each week. After your ninth and final official session, your relationship becomes less formal – you occasionally call by the café as you enjoy seeing Fiona's business grow. When your 16-year-old son is looking for a Saturday job, he is placed at the top of Fiona's waiting list.	

▶

Example 3. A networked opportunity	Observations
A former colleague contacts you to ask whether you might mentor one of their team who needs to build awareness of working across different cultures (that's something you have experience of). Ian is an experienced project manager, who is about to begin a project that involves working in Asia. You exchange CVs and schedule a meeting near your work location. When you meet, you spend time learning what you have in common, e.g. Ian's moving a young family to live abroad and you have done that. So you talk a little about the impact on marriage, kids and the effects of foreign schooling. What Ian is mainly interested in is how to build and lead teams in Asia as he finds the idea daunting.	This is a less structured relationship and so has potential flexibility but also risk, e.g. conversations may wander and lack true value.
You agree three areas to focus on: influence, building cross-cultural teams and working across global locations/time zones. You meet a few times before Ian leaves for Hong Kong and then have conversations over Skype every 6–8 weeks. While sometimes the conversations feel like chatting, you use the three focus areas to keep sight of what's relevant. You encourage Ian to learn about the region's history and culture as a way of demonstrating respect to his new colleagues. You also help him connect with a local ex-pat community, which his wife engages with. When you ask, Ian tells you that he's using the conversations to distinguish the real problems from imagined ones and has gained confidence in tackling those. Over time, your conversations become less frequent, e.g. once every six months.	It's important to make links early on to what you can specifically help with and trust that other areas of benefit will arise naturally.

The benefits of this assignment are most clearly for the mentee, Ian. As mentor you are fulfilled by contributing to someone else's success and by your broadened outlook arising from the conversations. |
| The relationship ends by Ian buying you dinner when he makes a return visit and you enjoy swapping stories and hearing about what's been happening. You keep in touch and enjoy receiving his occasional updates. | You trust that any additional benefits will be indirect, e.g. the goodwill of your former colleague. |

Appendix 3
Review an assignment: potential agenda topics and questions

No.	Topic and questions
1.	**The function of the meetings** • What works well about the way we're working together? (Frequency, duration and location of meetings, etc.) • What works less well? • What would work better?
2.	**Approach to the assignment** • How much is the level of structure we're using appropriate? (Agreements, expectations, identification of themes and objectives, etc.) • What might we do less of? (Formal agendas, meetings in person, etc.) • What could we add that would help? (Emailing notes, phone calls, etc.)

3.	**Progress, results and outcomes**
	• What have been the main results of mentoring support for you so far? For example:
	  ♦ What has happened that wouldn't have happened?
	  ♦ What has happened that has been affected/influenced by the mentoring?
	  ♦ What else seems relevant?
	• Considering what you hoped to get from mentoring, how successful/effective is it?
	• What hasn't the mentoring addressed that you feel is still a development need or barrier to your progress?

Appendix 4
Consolidate learning: potential agenda topics and questions

No.	Topic and questions
1.	**Review of progress made: since receiving mentoring support** • Thinking of your initial expectations and development goals, what progress do you feel you've made? • What areas have you made less progress in? ♦ What might be the cause of that? ♦ What other progress have you made? ♦ Progress that seems related. ♦ Progress that appears less related or unrelated.
2.	**Themes of the assignment: growth, wisdom and learning** • What are the ideas or messages that have arisen from mentor conversations? • What ideas do you think have been most important for you, i.e. that you want to remember the most? • How will these affect or influence you going forward? ♦ In the short term. ♦ In the longer term.
3.	**Exchange feedback: from mentee to mentor** • What do you see as your mentor's strengths in providing this type of support to people? • What do you value most about your mentor's support? • What might your mentor do/improve upon that would work better in future?

No.	Topic and questions
4.	**Exchange feedback: from mentor to mentee** • What do you see as your mentee's key strengths? • What do you value them for most? • What is their greatest potential contribution: ♦ In their role at work? ♦ Elsewhere (outside of their role, in life generally)? • What are their challenges (blocks of awareness, behaviour or ability)? ♦ What do they need to do in order to overcome those? ♦ What might be the benefits of that? • What else do you have to say?
5.	**Identify options for on-going support and learning** • What development themes does the mentee still have? (This may be the same as those used within the mentoring.) • How might the mentee continue to make progress? (Regular routines, training, etc.) • What support is available to them? (People, membership of networks, online resources and tools, etc.)
6.	**Agree a schedule to complete** • What needs to happen now before we complete? ♦ Actions (complete 'x' or finish 'y'). ♦ Activities, e.g. 'We'll have two more conversations, one in person and one by telephone.' ♦ Events, dates, milestones, e.g. wait until the mentee has spent six months in their new role.
7.	**Mentee summarises** • Confirm what's been agreed and the way forward.

Index